Contents

Foreword 5

Introduction 7

Land and cities 13

Past and present 47

The economy 75

Arts and living 91

The future 117

Almanac 120

Timeline 122

Glossary 124

Bibliography 125

Index 126

Foreword

Since ancient times, people have gathered together in communities where they could share and trade resources and strive to build a safe and happy environment. Gradually, as populations grew and societies became more complex, communities expanded to become nations – groups of people who felt sufficiently bound by a common heritage to work together for a shared future.

Land has usually played an important role in defining a nation. People have a natural affection for the landscape in which they grew up. They are proud of its natural beauties – the mountains, rivers and forests – and of the towns and cities that flourish there. People are proud, too, of their nation's history – the shared struggles and achievements that have shaped the way they live today.

Religion, culture, race and lifestyle, too, have sometimes played a role in fostering a nation's identity. Often, though, a nation includes people of different races, beliefs and customs. Many may have come from distant countries. Nations have rarely been fixed, unchanging things, either territorially or racially. Throughout history, borders have changed, often under the pressure of war, and people have migrated across the globe in search of a new life or because they are fleeing from oppression or disaster. The world's nations are still changing today: some nations are breaking up and new nations are forming.

As an island nation, Japan has been able to maintain a stable identity for many centuries, building a rich culture of great originality. Despite its isolation, however, Japan has been able to absorb cultural influences from overseas – from China, Korea and most recently from the West – without losing sight of its own traditions. In the early 20th century, like many other nations, Japan went through a period of extreme **nationalism**, during which its rulers attempted to create a vast Japanese empire in the Pacific. Today, though, Japan is a stable **democracy**, whose **constitution** explicitly forbids military aggression.

Introduction

Yōkoso – 'welcome' to Japan, a land where ancient and modern meet to make a unique culture. Modern Japan is one of the world's most advanced and wealthy nations. Despite its small size, it has the second-largest economy in the world in terms of its **gross national product** (GNP), after that of the USA. Today, Japan is best known for high-quality, high-tech goods, such as cars, computers, cameras and televisions – products that are assembled partly by robots in up-to-the-minute, modern factories.

Yet Japan is also a land where ancient religions and traditions are part of everyday life. Business people throng the streets in suits on weekdays, but put on **kimonos** – traditional robes tied with a sash – for festivals and holidays. In bustling cities, gleaming skyscrapers tower over historic shrines and temples. Out in the country, high-speed **bullet trains** race past a patchwork of golden rice (paddy) fields.

The country of Japan is made up of a chain of islands in the Pacific Ocean off the east coast of continental Asia. There are four main islands and thousands of smaller ones. From the coast, the land rises steeply to jagged mountain ranges with forest-covered slopes and snowy peaks. Japan is a land of great scenic beauty, with steaming hot springs, glittering lakes and thundering waterfalls. With frequent earthquakes, seasonal

Snow-capped Mount Fuji is one of Japan's most famous sights. The Japanese consider the mountain a holy place and a powerful symbol of their country.

The Japanese flag shows a red circle, symbolizing the sun, on a white background.

Everywhere you go in Japan, you will see these kanji, *or characters (right). They represent* Nippon *or* Nihon – *the Japanese name for the country.*

Japanese notes usually bear portraits of a famous author, scholar or emperor as well as traditional symbols, such as Mount Fuji.

typhoons (tropical hurricanes) and the occasional volcanic eruption, the country has more than its fair share of natural drama.

In the early years of its history, Japan was greatly influenced by its neighbours, Korea and, particularly, China. The traditional Japanese style of government, writing system, arts and architecture all owe much to ancient Chinese culture. About 150 years ago, however, Japan began to modernize rapidly, looking to Europe and the USA for inspiration. Today, Japanese culture is a unique blend of East and West. City restaurants serve hamburgers and pizzas as well as traditional dishes of fish and rice. Baseball and golf are popular national sports, as well as **sumo** (Japanese wrestling) and traditional martial arts.

Because Japan is so far east, the Japanese call their country *Nippon* or *Nihon*, which means 'source of the sun'. The English name 'Japan' is probably a European version of a Chinese word meaning 'land of the rising sun'.

Japan's currency is the yen, which is written ¥. There are 1, 5, 10, 50, 100 and 500-yen coins (two of which – the 5 and 500-yen coins – have a hole in the middle) and 1000, 5000 and 10,000-yen notes. Because Japan has such a low crime rate, most Japanese usually pay with cash and use credit cards only occasionally.

Japan is a parliamentary **democracy**. Like the United Kingdom's monarch (king or queen), the Japanese head of state – the emperor – has no real power. Japan's national flower, the chrysanthemum, is also the emperor's symbol.

POPULATION DENSITY

Japan is one of the most densely populated nations in the world. Most towns and cities are found along the coastal plains of the country's larger islands. Many cities have grown so big that they form a huge urban sprawl, or conurbation. By contrast, the mountainous areas inland are only sparsely populated and are havens for Japan's wildlife and plants.

PERSONS

Per sq km	Per sq mile
50	130
200	520
700	1810
2000	5200

TOKYO

Japan's population has risen steeply in the last 150 years.

PEOPLE AND POPULATION

Japan has a population of more than 126 million people. Its small land area means that it is one of the most crowded nations in the world. On average, there are 336 people per square kilometre (860 per square mile). This compares with 246 people per square kilometre (637 people per square mile) in the UK.

Japan's population is not evenly spread throughout the country, however. Most people live on narrow coastal plains, which are among the

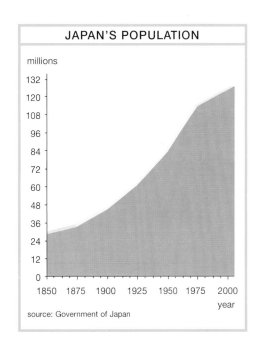

JAPAN'S POPULATION

millions

132
120
108
96
84
72
60
48
36
24
12
0

1850　1875　1900　1925　1950　1975　2000

year

source: Government of Japan

POPULATION BY AGE

%	
15.3	0–14 yrs
21.5	15–29 yrs
19.3	30-44 yrs
22.2	45-59 yrs
15.6	60-74 yrs
6.1	75+ yrs

source: Government of Japan

ETHNIC COMPOSITION

%	
98	Japanese
2	other

source: Government of Japan

RELIGIOUS PERSUASION

%	
90	Shinto and/or Buddhist
1.2	Christian
8.8	other

source: Government of Japan

The charts above show the composition of the Japanese population by age, ethnicity and religion.

most densely populated areas in the world. More than three-quarters of Japanese people live in towns and cities, leaving less than a quarter in the countryside. The total urban area of Japan's capital, Tokyo, has more than 26 million people and is the largest city in the world. The next largest Japanese city, Ōsaka, has 11 million inhabitants.

Japan's population is overwhelmingly Japanese – 98 per cent. Koreans make up most of the remainder (0.6 per cent), with Chinese forming 0.2 per cent. These people are largely immigrants who have come to Japan to find work or new opportunities. A people called the **Ainu** are thought to be some of Japan's earliest inhabitants, but today there are only some 14,000 Ainu left in Japan. Intermarriage between the Japanese and the Ainu is common, and experts calculate that as few as 200 people are pure-blooded Ainu people. The vast majority of this ancient and dwindling people live on the island of Hokkaidō in the north of Japan.

The Japanese are the longest-living people in the world, with women expecting to reach the age of 85, and men 78. Today, 23 per cent of Japan's population are over the age of 65, with a relatively low figure, 15.3 per cent, under the age of fourteen. The Japanese government is concerned that the economy will be unable to support a large non-working older population (see page 119).

This chart shows that the Japanese population is overwhelmingly urban.

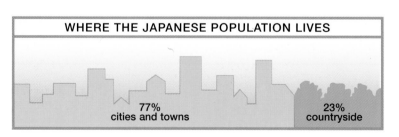

WHERE THE JAPANESE POPULATION LIVES

77%
cities and towns

23%
countryside

LANGUAGE AND RELIGION

Japan's official language, Japanese, has many local dialects (forms). The standard spoken dialect is that of Tokyo. The traditional Japanese system of writing is based not on an alphabet but on characters called *kanji*. There are several thousand *kanji*, each representing a different word. The *kanji* were originally based on Chinese characters. Over the centuries, however, they have come to look very different from their Chinese ancestors (see page 108).

The main religions of Japan are **Shinto** and **Buddhism**. Shinto, which means 'the way of the gods', is a very ancient faith. Buddhism, too, was introduced more than 1500 years ago. In Japan, most people follow both religions – 90 per cent of the population follow Shinto and 75 per cent are Buddhists – and Buddhist temples are often found close to Shinto shrines. Christians make up just over 1 per cent of the population. In addition, there are a variety of new religions that often blend elements from older religions and beliefs.

The national anthem

The national anthem is called 'Kimigayo', which means 'Our Emperor's Reign'. The words of the anthem are taken from a 1000-year-old poem and were set to music in 1880 to celebrate the birthday of Emperor Meiji. The composer, Hiromori Hayashi, was a musician at the emperor's court. The song became Japan's national anthem in 1888.

Ten thousand years of happy reign be yours.
Rule on, my lord, till what are pebbles now
By ages united to mighty rocks shall grow
On whose venerable sides the moss does grow.

How Japanese is written in this book

Modern Japanese is sometimes written using the Roman alphabet, called *romaji* in Japanese. Most of the *romaji* letters used to represent Japanese sounds are pronounced much as they are in English. A few have a special pronunciation:

f	pronounced while pursing the lips
l	pronounced more like *r*
g	pronounced like *g* in 'gate' at the beginning of a word but like *ng* in the middle.

Some vowels, too, are 'long'; that is, the sound is held twice as long as a normal vowel. A long vowel is indicated by a bar (macron) over the letter – for example, a long *o* is written as ō.

Land and cities

*'The extreme part of the known world unto us is the noble
island Japan … This country is hilly and pestered with snow.'*

A 16th-century Englishman's description of Japan

Japan is an island nation in the north Pacific Ocean,
situated about 500 kilometres (310 miles) off the
mainland of Asia. To the west, across the Sea of Japan,
lie the Russian Federation, China and Korea. To the east
lie the vast waters of the Pacific Ocean, with Canada
and the USA some 7200 kilometres (4500 miles) away.

There are four main islands. Furthest north is
Hokkaidō, of which the northern tip is separated from
the Russian island of Sakhalin by a narrow strait. To the
south of Hokkaidō is Honshū, which is by far the largest
island. Two other large islands, Shikoku and Kyushū, lie
south-west of Honshū across the Inland Sea.

Together, the four main islands make up an arc that
curves through more than 15 degrees of latitude, from
30° N to 45° N – the distance between northern Italy
and Libya. In addition to the four main islands, there
are some 3900 smaller ones. Two island groups, the
Rykūyū and the Bonin islands, dot the ocean to the
south of the large islands.

The greatest distance from west to east in Japan is
less than 320 kilometres (200 miles), but from the north
to the south, the country stretches 2250 kilometres
(1400 miles). The great distance from north to south
means the scenery and climate of Japan vary dramati-
cally, from frozen wastes and ice floes in the north to
tropical islands and coral reefs in the south.

*Tokyo's Imperial Palace can be visited on only two days of the year. The rest
of the year, the palace can be glimpsed from the Nijū-bashi Bridge.*

FACT FILE

● Cities that stand
at a comparable
latitude to Japan's
most northerly and
southerly points are
Bucharest (Romania)
and Cairo (Egypt).

● Japan stands
in one of the Earth's
most volcanic
zones, with some
65 active
volcanoes. The
country also lies
in the west Pacific
earthquake belt
and has suffered
many devastating
shocks, notably in
1923 and 1995.

● Japan's rugged
coastline measures
an astonishing
29,800 km (18,500
miles).

● Tokyo has lower
average January
temperatures than
Reykjavík, the
capital of Iceland.

A huge plume of ash erupts from the summit of Mount Sakura-jima in Kyūshū.

The Japanese believe that mountains are sacred places, and volcanoes such as Mount Fuji have long been worshipped for their power.

THE TERRAIN

The islands of Japan are actually the tops of a great range of undersea mountains that rise from the floor of the Pacific Ocean. At one time, Japan was connected to mainland Asia. At the end of the last Ice Age, some 10,000 years ago, the sea level rose and formed the Sea of Japan that today separates Japan from the mainland.

Some 80 per cent of Japan is mountainous. The mountains are covered with forests and dotted with sparkling lakes. Swift-flowing rivers cut through the ranges, forming craggy gorges. From the high ground inland, short, fast-flowing rivers tumble down to the sea.

A land of volcanoes

Many of Japan's mountains are volcanoes, including Mount Fuji (see page 21), the country's highest point at 3776 metres (12,388 feet). There are more than 180 volcanoes, 65 of which are still active. Mount Sakura-

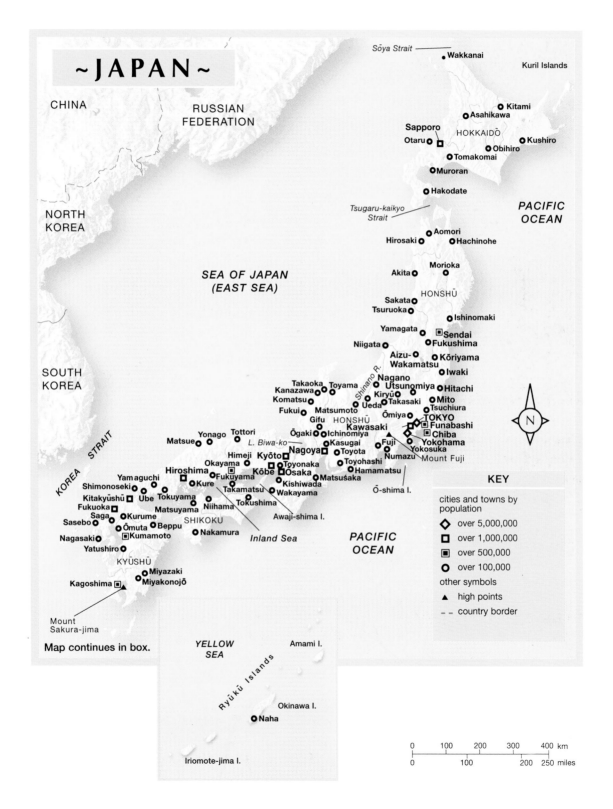

~JAPAN~

CHINA

RUSSIAN FEDERATION

NORTH KOREA

SOUTH KOREA

KOREA STRAIT

SEA OF JAPAN (EAST SEA)

Sōya Strait
• Wakkanai
Kuril Islands

• Kitami
Asahikawa
Sapporo
Otaru
HOKKAIDŌ
• Kushiro
Obihiro
Tomakomai
Muroran

Hakodate

PACIFIC OCEAN

Tsugaru-kaikyo Strait

Aomori
Hirosaki
Hachinohe

Akita
Morioka

HONSHŪ

Sakata
Tsuruoka
Ishinomaki

Yamagata
Sendai
Niigata
Fukushima

Aizu-Wakamatsu
Kōriyama
Iwaki

Takaoka
Nagano
Kanazawa
Toyama
Utsunomiya
Hitachi
Komatsu
Kiryū
Takasaki
Mito
Fukui
Matsumoto
Ueda
Tsuchiura
Gifu
HONSHŪ
Ōmiya
TOKYO
Ōgaki
Ichinomiya
Kawasaki
Funabashi
Chiba
Yonago
Tottori
Kasugai
Yokohama
Matsue
L. Biwa-ko
Nagoya
Fuji
Yokosuka
Himeji
Kyōto
Toyota
Numazu
Okayama
Kōbe
Toyohashi
Mount Fuji
Hiroshima
Osaka
Hamamatsu
Fukuyama
Kure
Matsusaka
Yamaguchi
Takamatsu
Kishiwada
Shimonoseki
Wakayama
Ō-shima I.
Kitakyūshū
Ube
Tokuyama
Niihama
Fukuoka
Matsuyama
Tokushima
Saga
Kurume
SHIKOKU
Sasebo
Ōmuta
Beppu
Awaji-shima I.
Nagasaki
Kumamoto
Nakamura
Inland Sea
Yatushiro

Shinano R.

PACIFIC OCEAN

KEY

cities and towns by population

◆ over 5,000,000
□ over 1,000,000
▣ over 500,000
○ over 100,000

other symbols

▲ high points
-- country border

KYŪSHŪ
Miyazaki
Miyakonojō
Kagoshima

Mount Sakura-jima

Map continues in box.

YELLOW SEA
Amami I.

Ryūkū Islands

Okinawa I.
• Naha

Iriomote-jima I.

| 0 | 100 | 200 | 300 | 400 km |
| 0 | | 100 | | 200 250 miles |

of the crust was forced upwards to form the craggy islands of Japan. The islands were further shaped by volcanoes, as molten rock from deep inside the Earth forced its way through weak points in the crust, gushing out to form landscapes of lava.

Today, the tremendous forces that created Japan are still at work. The islands contain one-tenth of the world's active volcanoes, and from time to time, there is a major eruption. Japan's volcanoes do not erupt often, however. Earthquakes, caused by shifts in the Earth's crust, are far more common. Quakes occur daily, but most are minor tremors too small to be noticed. Every now and then, there is a major quake. Out at sea an earthquake can cause a tsunami (tidal wave). When these giant walls of water reach land, they damage ports and flood coastal areas.

The city of Kōbe lies close to the centre of an earthquake zone. On 17 January 1995, a major earthquake devastated the city. Some 6000 people died, and many buildings (like the one shown in the photo here) collapsed.

Nowadays, Japan spends billions of yen each year on earthquake research in an effort to predict major quakes before they happen. That way, cities can be evacuated and many lives saved. In Japanese cities, buildings are designed to stand up to all but the largest quakes.

The shifting Earth

The origins of the islands of Japan lie in movements of the Earth's vast tectonic plates – the rigid pieces that make up the Earth's outer shell. Japan lies in a region where two of these great plates meet and grind against one another. Over millions of years, the island chain of Japan formed where the Asian plate met and slowly collided with the Pacific plate. Enormous pressure caused the edges of the plates to buckle, and part jima on Kyūshū regularly belches smoke and rains ash down on the surrounding region. People living in towns near the volcano are used to washing ash from their cars almost every week. In 1986, Mount Mihara on Ō-shima Island, near Tokyo, erupted. Thousands of people living nearby had to be evacuated.

The coastal plains

Since the mountains are too steep for building and farming, most people live on the flat plains along the coasts or in narrow valleys. The fertile soil of the plains is made of fragments from the mountains, carried down by fast-flowing streams and rivers, and of sediment from the sea.

Although only 15 per cent of Japan is low-lying, 80 per cent of the population live in the lowlands. Cities, factories and farmlands are all crowded into coastal strips. Space is so tight that land has to be reclaimed from the sea. The largest lowland area is the Kantō Plain, on Honshū, where Tokyo stands.

Japanese place names

On a map of Japan, you will often find that place names are followed by a hyphen plus a suffix (a word ending). The suffix indicates what kind of place it is. For example, the name Tanega-shima means Tanega Island.

A few other suffixes you will come across in this book are: -wan (bay), -san (mountain), -hanto (peninsula), -ko (lake) and -ji (Buddhist temple). In this book, the full Japanese name is followed by a translation of the kind of place – for example, Tanega-shima Island.

Rivers and lakes

Japan's rivers are short and fast-flowing. The longest river in Japan, the Shinano, flows just 367 kilometres (228 miles) from the mountains of central Honshū down to the Sea of Japan. Japan's largest freshwater lake, Biwa-ko, is also on Honshū, north-east of Kyoto, and covers some 672 square kilometres (259 square miles).

Japan's rivers and lakes have difficulty meeting the population's growing demand for fresh water. Japan has few natural reservoirs, and engineers find it difficult to build large dams in the rugged inland mountains.

REGIONS AND PREFECTURES OF JAPAN

Japan is divided into nine regions, called **chihō**, and further divided into 47 smaller divisions. Of these smaller areas, 43 are **ken**, known as prefectures in English. The remaining four are Tokyo, which has the status of *to* (capital), Ōsaka and Kyōto, which are *fu* (urban prefectures), and Hokkaidō, which is a *dō* (district).

Listed below are the names of the prefectures and other divisions together with their capital (marked on the map with a dot). In Japanese, the names of the *ken* are written Fukui-ken, Aichi-ken and so on.

KEN (PREFECTURES)

1 AOMORI Aomori
2 AKITA Akita
3 IWATE Morioka
4 MIYAGI Sendai
5 YAMAGATA Yamagata
6 FUKUSHIMA Fukishima
7 IBARAKI Mito
8 TOCHIGI Utsunomiya
9 GUMMA Maebashi
10 SAITAMA Urawa
11 CHIBA Chiba
12 KANAGAWA Yokohama
13 NIIGATA Niigata
14 YAMANASHI Kōfu
15 SHIZUOKA Shizuoka
16 NAGANO Nagano
17 TOYAMA Toyama
18 ISHIKAWA Kanazawa
19 FUKUI Fukui
20 GIFU Gifu
21 AICHI Nagoya
22 MIE Tsu
23 SHIGA Ōtsu
24 NARA Nara
25 WAKAYAMA Wakayama
26 HYŌGO Kōbe
27 KAGAWA Takamatsu
28 TOKUSHIMA Tokushima
29 KŌCHI Kōchi
30 EHIME Matsuyama
31 TOTTORI Tottori
32 OKAYAMA Okayama

33 HIROSHIMA Hiroshima
34 SHIMANE Matsue
35 YAMAGUCHI Yamaguchi
36 NAGASAKI Nagasaki
37 SAGA Saga
38 FUKUOKA Fukuoka
39 ŌITA Ōita
40 KUMAMOTO Kumamoto
41 MIYAZAKI Miyazaki
42 KAGOSHIMA Kagoshima
43 OKINAWA Naha

DŌ (DISTRICTS)
HOKKAIDŌ Sapporo

FU (URBAN PREFECTURES)
29 ŌSAKA-FU Ōsaka
26 KYŌTO-FU Kyōto

TŌ (CAPITAL)
TOKYO-TŌ Tokyo

HOKKAIDŌ
Hokkaidō-dō

TOHOKU

KANTŌ

CHŪBU

KINKI

Kyōto-fu

Ōsaka-fu

Tokyo-tō

CHUGOKU

SHIKOKU

KYŪSHŪ

Map continues right.

Continuation of main map

KYŪSHŪ

OKINAWA

18

THE REGIONS OF JAPAN

Throughout Japan's history, its rulers have divided the country in many different ways. Usually the country's political boundaries have been determined by its geography – by seas and by mountains. For example, 1000 years ago, the island of Honshū was divided into two. The lowlands west of the mountains that run down its middle were Kansai and those to the east were Kanto.

Today, Japan is divided into nine regions. Each of the four main islands forms its own region, except the largest, Honshū, which is divided into five. The island of Okinawa and the surrounding islands form another region. Each of the regions has its own special character.

Hokkaidō: a land of snows

Hokkaidō is the most northerly of Japan's main islands. It is on the same latitude as northern Italy and has a colder climate than the rest of Japan. During the long, harsh winters, snow may cover the ground for up to four months. With an area of 77,900 square kilometres (30,077 square miles), it is Japan's second-largest island, but it is home to only 5 per cent of Japan's population. Hokkaidō used to be regarded as a very remote region and very few people lived there. Only the **Ainu** (see page 50), some of the earliest inhabitants of Japan, were at home there.

Hokkaidō is diamond shaped with a hilly peninsula that curves south. Off the north-east coast, the Kuril Islands are part of Russia, but Japan also claims them (see page 69). Hokkaidō's economy is based on dairy farming, fishing, forestry and tourism. The dairy industry flourishes here because there is lots of land suitable for grazing cows.

This is the kanji for ken (prefecture).

This farm lies high up in the mountains of Hokkaidō. Heavy snows occur in the region, and the steep-sided roofs help the snow to slide off.

Central Hokkaidō is mountainous and mainly undeveloped. Bear and deer roam forested mountain slopes, and sheep and cattle graze high moorland pastures. Daisetsuzan National Park (see page 32) is the largest wilderness area in Japan. The park is popular with tourists who want to walk, ski or just enjoy the rugged scenery.

Hokkaidō's largest lowland area is the Ishikari Plain in the south-west. The city of Sapporo on the plain is Hokkaidō's capital and Japan's fifth-largest city. Unlike many other Japanese cities, Sapporo was carefully planned on a grid system with wide avenues, built with help from US advisers sent at the request of the governor of Hokkaidō in 1870. It is a popular ski resort and hosted the Winter Olympic Games in 1972. Every February, people flock to the Sapporo Snow Festival. There they can enjoy winter sports or marvel at fantastic statues of animals and buildings carved from ice.

In the south-west of the island, the Seikan Tunnel crosses the Tsugaru-kaikyo Strait, running under the sea for over 53 kilometres (33 miles). It links Hokkaidō with Honshū and is the world's second-longest tunnel, after the Channel Tunnel, which links France and the United Kingdom.

Honshū: Japan's 'mainland'

Honshū is Japan's largest island, and the Japanese think of it as the 'mainland'. Shaped like a boomerang, it curves to the south-west towards Korea. Nowhere on Honshū is more than 120 kilometres (75 miles) from the coast. With an area of 230,831 square kilometres (89,124 square miles), the island is home to some 80 per cent of the Japanese people.

Northern Honshū is the least-developed part of the island and has the harshest climate. Jagged mountain ranges run down the middle, with narrow coastal plains on either side. In central Honshū, three mountain ranges known as the Japanese Alps form the highest mountains in Japan. East of these mountains is a chain of volcanoes, which includes Mount Fuji (see box opposite).

These are the kanji for Mount Fuji – Japan's holy mountain – which is located on Honshū.

Mount Fuji: Japan's holy mountain

The perfect, snow-capped cone of the volcano Mount Fuji is one of Japan's most powerful symbols (see page 6). Serene and snow-covered for most of the year, its beauty has been a subject of Japanese art for hundreds of years. The woodblock print above, for example, is part of a series of pictures of the mountain by the famous Japanese artist Katsushika Hokusai (see page 94). On a clear winter's day, Mount Fuji can be seen from Tokyo 100 km (60 miles) to the north-east.

There are different ideas about what the mountain's name means. Some say it means 'everlasting'; others say the name comes from the Ainu language and means 'fire'. Japanese people revere the mountain greatly. Some believe that the mountain has a soul. Every July and August, thousands of pilgrims climb the mountain to visit its many temples or to watch the sun rise over the summit.

Mount Fuji in fact consists of three volcanoes, although lava from one – Shin Fuji (New Fuji) – has covered the other two and they can no longer be seen. Mount Fuji is dormant (inactive). It last erupted in 1707, scattering ash as far away as Tokyo.

In the north of Honshū is the Tohoku region. This remote and mountainous region has changed less quickly than many other parts of Japan. It was only in the 17th century that the area came under central government control. Life in its mountain villages, country towns and hot-spring resorts is very traditional. There are few large industrial areas or major ports, and people often leave the region to find work. Those who remain make a living from farming – growing rice or raising cattle – or forestry.

The largest city, Sendai, has a population of more than 900,000. It is a modern city with broad boulevards and an efficient underground railway system. Sendai is full of students who attend the city's eight universities.

The lowlands of the central Kantō and Chūbu regions are the most developed part of Honshū. In the east, the large Kantō Plain slopes down to Tokyo Bay. It is the site of a vast urban area where Japan's capital, Tokyo (see pages 33–9), merges into the cities of Kawasaki and Yokohama. Away from Tokyo are ancient religious sites such as Nikkō and Kamakura. Nikkō lies 137 kilometres (85 miles) north of the capital. It is a collection of important religious shrines and temples, set against a backdrop of giant cedars more than 400 years old. The roofs and walls of the buildings are decorated with intricate carvings of animals and birds.

The coastal strip south from Tokyo to Yokohama is the most densely populated part of Japan. The cities here look much like American cities, with towering skyscrapers and broad streets. Beyond Mount Fuji and into Shizuoka prefecture, rows of neat, green bushes ring the hillsides, forming the large plantations that produce Japan's finest teas. The next major city is Nagoya, an important industrial centre. At the nearby city of Toyota, cars are manufactured; other factories produce chemicals and textile machines.

In the centre of Honshū are the Japanese Alps where people visit ski resorts in winter. After a day spent skiing, they often go to nearby hot-spring resorts (see box opposite) and relax in a hot spring. In summer, the mountains around Matsumoto attract walkers and climbers.

In Kōbe, a cable car takes visitors up Mount Rokko, from where there is a spectacular view over the city's harbour.

Natural hot springs

Japan's volcanic terrain has one big advantage: the hot springs (*onsen*) that bubble up from deep within the Earth where water is heated by molten rock. Resorts have grown up around the springs, and visitors come to bathe and relax in the steaming waters.

According to legend, the first baths were founded at Dogo Onsen, near Matsuyama, almost 3000 years ago. Over the centuries, many famous people came to relax at the resort, including some of the earliest emperors, great Buddhist teachers, poets and novelists. The present bathhouse was built in the Meiji period (1868–1912). It has a spectacular roof that rises in several tiers with upward-curving eaves. As visitors

walk the short distance from their hotels to the hot springs, the *geta* (Japanese clogs) they wear make a clattering sound on the cobblestoned streets.

Inside the bathhouse, visitors change into a *yukata*, something like a light cotton **kimono**, then make their way into the ancient stone baths. Sitting on wooden stools, they wash carefully, rinse off the soap then get into the bath and relax in the bubbling hot water. The *onsen* water is known to relieve physical ailments such as rheumatism and arthritis, but most people visit the baths to relax their bodies and unwind from the stresses of work. The resort of Beppu, Kyūshū, shown above, is one of Japan's most popular *onsen* resorts.

At high tide, the sea floods the gateway (torii) to the Itsukushima shrine on Mija-jima Island, southern Honshū. In early times, the island was sacred and people could not walk on it. To visit the temple, they had to approach the shrine from the sea, entering through the 'floating' gateway.

On Honshū's north-western coast are two historical cities – Kanazawa and Toyama. Kanazawa's old winding streets and alleys are lined with traditional homes and shops. It is a well-known centre for arts, where local people perform in traditional **Noh** theatre (see page 97) and comedy plays. Toyama has also been an important centre for oriental medicine since the 17th century.

To the south-west, in Kinki region, the cities of Ōsaka and Kōbe stand on the Ōsaka Plain. Together with Kyōto, they form a triangular industrial area, second in importance only to the Tokyo–Yokohama area. Ōsaka is Japan's third-largest city and home to Japan's puppet theatre, called *bunraku* (see pages 97–8). The ancient capitals, Kyōto (see pages 42–3) and Nara, lie close by. Lake Biwa-ko, Japan's largest lake, is only a short distance from Kyōto. It is shaped like the musical instrument called a *biwa*, from where it gets its name.

South-western Honshū – Chūgoku – is divided into two parts by the Chūgoku Mountains, which run from east to west. The coast of San-in, the northern part, is battered by the Sea of Japan. San-yo, the area south of the mountains, is on the Inland Sea and has a milder climate. Cities and farmlands are set in small pockets of lowland.

The city of Hiroshima (see pages 44–5), towards the southern end of Honshū, stands on a large bay. In the bay, the beautiful island of Miya-jima has a very famous shrine. A graceful red gateway (*torii*) to the shrine stands in the sea. At the southern tip of Honshū is Shimonoseki, a seaport and industrial city, which is linked by a tunnel to Kitakyūshū in Kyūshū.

Shikoku

Shikoku, Japan's smallest main island, lies off the south coast of western Honshū, across the Inland Sea. With an area of 18,798 square kilometres (7258 square miles), the island is home to just 3 per cent of Japan's population. Until recent times, Shikoku was known as a quiet backwater. Today, however, three major bridge networks connect Shikoku with Honshū (see pages 88–9).

Although it has a mild climate, Shikoku is relatively undeveloped. Mountain ranges run from west to east across the island, making inland areas hard to reach. There are no major lowland areas, and towns, industrial centres and farmlands are all crowded into narrow coastal strips. The largest cities – Matsuyama, Takamatsu and Tokushima – are on the northern coast. Rice, wheat, oranges and tobacco are grown along the coast on land not occupied by factories or towns.

Shikoku is a popular **pilgrimage** centre. On the island are 88 temples built in honour of Kūkai, a **Buddhist** monk who was born on Shikoku in 774. Kūkai helped introduce the Buddhist religion to Japan and was honoured as a Buddhist saint. Spring is the favourite season for making the pilgrimage. Pilgrims dress in a white kimono, leggings and mittens. Some make the pilgrimage on foot, taking two months to walk round the 88 temples, while others go by bus and finish in two weeks.

On the east coast of Shikoku is a spectacular natural feature – the Naruto Whirlpools. These form in the narrow channel that separates Shikoku from Awajishima Island. A difference in the sea level on each side of the channel pulls the tides into a whirling mass of water that breaks on the rocks along the coast.

The Seto–Chuo Expressway connecting northern Shikoku with Honshū was opened in 1988. In fact, it is a series of six bridges and four viaducts that hop from island to island across the Inland Sea. Altogether, the bridges span some 12 kilometres (7 1/2 miles).

The longest single-span suspension bridge in the world is in Japan. The Akashi Kaikyō Bridge connects southeast Honshū with Awaji-shima Island.

Kyūshū: 'Silicon Island'

Kyūshū is Japan's most southern main island. With an area of 44,380 square kilometres (17,135 square miles), it is the third-largest island in Japan and is home to 11 per cent of the population. After Honshū, it is the most developed island. Kyūshū has the nickname 'Silicon Island' because of its computer and microchip industry.

Four mountain ranges run north to south across the island. The enormous Mount Aso volcano caldera (crater) lies in the north-east, at the heart of a beautiful national park. The mountain has five summits and the largest caldera in the world. The central peak, Mount Nakadake, is an active volcano that regularly billows smoke. East of the national park, the port of Beppu is famous for its hot springs (see page 23).

Kyūshū enjoys a semi-tropical climate, with long, hot summers and mild winters. Its jagged western shore is dotted with islands. The port of Nagasaki lies on the west coast. From the 17th century to the mid-19th, when the rest of Japan was closed to foreigners, Nagasaki was visited by Dutch traders. Gradually, Nagasaki became an important centre for trade and Western learning. In

Most of Kyūshū's population lives on the narrow strips of lowland between the sea and the inland mountains. Here wheat fields lie in a patchwork pattern on the land along the shore of Isahaya Bay.

1945, the city was the target of the second **atomic bomb** dropped by the USA.

Most of Kyūshū's population lives on small patches of lowland in the north and west. The largest cities, Fukuoka and Kitakyūshū, lie on the north coast. At the Kanmon Strait, near Kitakyūshū, only 1.6 kilometres (1 mile) of water separate Kyūshū from Honshū. Road and rail tunnels under the strait carry traffic between the two.

The Ryūkū kingdom

Until the 1870s, the Ryūkū Islands were an independent kingdom. In the 15th century, the Ryūkū kings united all the islands for the first time and ruled the kingdom from Shuri Castle in Okinawa's present-day capital, Naha. The Ryūkū people were peaceful traders and they had their own colourful culture, influenced by nearby Chinese Taiwan.

In 1609, however, a Japanese clan from southern Kyūshū invaded the islands and the Ryūkū kings became its vassals. In the late 19th century, Japan formally annexed Okinawa and set up military bases on the islands.

Smaller islands

The Ryūkyū and the Bonins are two groups of islands that lie south of the main islands of Japan. The Ryūkyū Islands are a chain of some 100 craggy islands that stretch some 1130 kilometres (700 miles) from Kyūshū, almost to Taiwan. They have a subtropical climate with lush vegetation. Altogether, the Ryūkyū are home to about 1 million people. Tourists flock there to enjoy the sandy beaches and to dive or snorkel in the clear, blue waters around the islands' coral reefs.

Okinawa in the southern Ryūkyū is the largest island, with an area of 1166 square kilometres (450 square miles), and is a region in its own right. In the 19th century, the martial art of karate originated on Okinawa. After World War Two, the Ryūkyū Islands were occupied by the USA. The northern group was returned to Japan in 1953, and the southern group in 1972. There are still a number of US military bases on the islands.

The Bonin Islands, a group of 97 islands, lie 970 kilometres (600 miles) south-east of Japan. They were occupied by US forces in 1945 but were returned in 1968. Crops of sugar cane, bananas and pineapples are grown.

The most southern islands of Okinawa prefecture – and of Japan – are the Yaeyama Islands, which lie just north of the Tropic of Cancer.

JAPAN'S CLIMATE

The Japanese are fascinated by their country's weather. After greeting one another, people almost always talk about the weather and the changing seasons.

The enormous north–south range of Japan's territory means that the country encompasses very different climates. In the far north, Hokkaidō's climate is like Siberia's, with short, cool summers and long, cold and snowy winters. Temperatures in winter may fall as low as −10 °C (14 °F), while on a warm summer day, the temperature may rise to 23 °C (73 °F).

In Okinawa, in the Ryūkyū Islands in the far south, the climate is subtropical, with hot summers and warm winters. Summers are scorching, with temperatures as high as 32 °C (90 °F), while winter temperatures rarely fall below 10 °C (50 °F). Temperatures also fall with altitude, so the peaks of high mountains are often many degrees lower than the lowlands below.

Japan's position between the Pacific Ocean and the Asian land mass, together with the great north–south length of the archipelago, create a very complex climate. Sapporo, on the west coast of Hokkaidō, has long, snowy winters. Tokyo, by contrast, has very cold winters but hardly any snow.

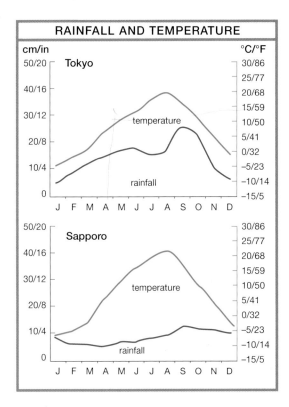

RAINFALL AND TEMPERATURE

Tokyo

Sapporo

Monsoons and currents

Monsoons are seasonal winds that bring different weather to western and eastern parts of Japan. In winter, cold winds blowing from north-west Asia bring cool air to northern Japan and cause rain and snow to fall on western coasts. In summer, moist winds from the Pacific make southern and central areas hot and humid.

Ocean currents also affect Japan's climate. The Japan Current is a warm sea current that flows east along southern coasts as far as Tokyo Bay, warming the land. Another warm current, the Kuroshio Current, flows along western shores. In winter it warms the air, but it also increases rainfall. Further north, the cold Oyashio Current flows down from the Arctic to cool the eastern shore of Hokkaidō. Fogs often form where the current meets warmer waters flowing from the south.

The seasons

Because Japan is situated in the Northern Hemisphere, its seasons fall at roughly the same time as they do in Europe and the USA. December to February are the coldest months. The arrival of spring is marked by the blossoming of cherry trees. All over Japan, people celebrate the cherry blossoms with a festival called *hanami*, meaning 'flower viewing'. Families gather to picnic on mats spread beneath the flowering branches.

Cherry blossom time is followed by a rainy season that lasts about two months. Summers are hot and humid, with temperatures highest in August. Many Japanese leave the scorching cities at this time and head for the cool of the mountains.

Autumn is the season of typhoons. These tropical storms sweep in from the Pacific, bringing torrential rains and rough seas to the south-east. As many as 30 typhoons may hit Japan each year, uprooting trees and wrecking ships and houses. The strong winds of up to 200 kilometres per hour (125 miles per hour) mostly blow themselves out before they reach the Tokyo Plain.

The stormy season is followed by a period of mild, clear weather in October and early November. Many tourists choose to visit Japan at this time, as autumn turns the trees to a blaze of colour, and before the winter chill sets in. Autumn is another time when the Japanese traditionally enjoy the colours of nature.

Women in traditional dress shelter under umbrellas as they leave a Shinto shrine. Japan gets plenty of rainfall. Almost everywhere in Japan, there are more than 100 centimetres (40 inches) of rain each year, with most rain falling in late spring and autumn.

WILDLIFE AND PLANTS

The great north–south distance in Japan means that a huge variety of plants and animals live there, including both tropical and Arctic species. Some 17,000 plant species are found among Japan's rich vegetation.

A land of trees and flowers

Forests cover 68 per cent of the land in Japan. On hills and mountains, many native plants survive, but in the lowlands, natural vegetation has been replaced by farm-land and cities. Different trees exist in various regions. In southern Japan, palm and camphor trees and tree ferns flourish. Bamboo groves sprout in river valleys, and subtropical coasts are surrounded by mangrove swamps.

In temperate central Honshū, red cedar trees are prized for timber. Broadleaved species include oak, chestnut, beech and maple. Further north, broadleaved forests give way to evergreens. On Hokkaidō, conifer (cone-bearing) trees dominate, includ-ing spruce, larch and fir.

All over Japan, the seasonal flowering of well-loved plants is greeted with festivals and celebrations. Cherry and other fruit trees blossom in spring. Lotus flowers bloom in August, and the chrysan-themum, the imperial and national flower, appears in November.

The sika is a species of deer found in the forests of east Asia. The Japanese sika is the smallest kind, just 80–86 centimetres (30–34 inches) to the shoulder. In winter, the sika's coat is grey brown, and in summer, it is reddish with brown spots.

Mammals and birds

Japan's animals are less varied than its plants, but the islands are still home to 140 different mammal species, 450 bird species and many reptiles and insects. Common mam-mals include foxes, badgers, squirrels, mice and bats. Graceful sika deer have reddish coats spot-ted with brown in summer and darker fur in winter. The red-faced monkey, or Japanese macaque, is also common. In northern Honshū, troops of macaques keep warm in winter by bathing in hot springs.

Japan's birds include many waterbirds, including cranes, herons, swans, ducks and cormorants. Land birds include sparrows, swallows, thrushes, nightingales and robins. The giant salamander of Japan is the largest amphibian in the world.

The steamy south and snowy north have their own animal species. The Ryūkyū Islands, south of Kyūhū, are home to the Ryūkyū rabbit and the rare spiny mouse. Tropical fish and deadly sea snakes swim in the warm waters among the coral reefs. In the north of Japan, Hokkaidō is home to red deer, brown bears and subarctic birds such as ravens and eagle owls.

The environment

Japan does not have a good reputation in environmental matters and is a regular target for environmental groups such as Greenpeace. Japan, along with Iceland and Norway, is one of the world's three countries that permit whaling. Dolphins regularly fall prey to the widespread Japanese practice of drift net fishing, and every year some 30,000 hawksbill turtles, an endangered species, are slaughtered for their valuable shells.

Japanese macaques, sometimes known as snow monkeys, have thick, rugged fur to protect them from the icy cold of Honshū. The macaques also like to keep warm by bathing in the region's hot springs.

Drift net fishing involves two boats, which may be anything up to 50 kilometres (30 miles) apart, hauling a fine net between them and catching everything – from tuna to dolphin – in their path.

JAPAN'S NATIONAL PARKS

Japan's national parks are found throughout the country, from the northern tips of Hokkaidō (Shiretoko and Rishiri-Rebun-Sarobetsu national parks) to the most southerly islands (Iriomote-jima Island). They include unspoiled coastlines (Kirishima-Yaku), volcanoes (Kirishima), lakes and forests (Akan), lonely islands (Inland Sea) and swamp land (Kushiro Shitsugen). The largest of the parks is the Daisetsuzan National Park in Hokkaidō, which covers some 2310 square kilometres (890 square miles) of forest, lakes and volcanoes.

Rishiri-Rebun-Sarobetsu

Shiretoko

HOKKAIDŌ

Akan

Daisetsuzan

Shikotsu-Tōya

Kushiro Shitsugen

Towada-Hachimantai

Bandai-Asahi

Rikuchu Kaigan

Nikkō

Chūbu Sangaku

HONSHŪ

Hakusan

Jōshin-Etsu-Kōgen

Inland Sea

Chichibu-Tama

Aso-Kujuu

Minami-Alps

Ise-Shima

Saikai

Yoshino-Kumano

Fuji-Hakone-Izu

Unzen Amakusa

KYŪSHŪ

SHIKOKU

Kirishima

Kyūshū-Chūōsanchi

Kirishima-Yaku

Iriomote-jima Island

Japan is also the world's biggest consumer of tropical rainforest timber. A great deal of the wood goes to produce disposable chopsticks (*waribashi*) for Japan's restaurants and noodle bars. Japan's own forests, too, are falling prey to pollution, acid rain and the spread of towns and cities.

The cramped conditions on Japanese islands means that many species that were once common are now at risk of dying out altogether. The crested ibis, once a familiar sight, is now close to extinction, as is the Japanese crane. Brown bears once roamed forests throughout Japan. This powerful bear can grow to a height of more than 2 metres (6 feet). Now they have been hunted to extinction, except on Hokkaidō, where only a few hundred bears remain.

Despite this neglect of the environment, Japan does have a large number of national parks. These were set up to help preserve the wild areas of Japan, particularly in the far north and the far south of the country.

THE CITIES

Japan's population lives overwhelmingly in towns and cities. Sometimes the cities are so close to one another that they merge, creating vast urban sprawls. Japan's big cities are vibrant places, full of energy and colour. New, exciting buildings are always appearing on their skylines, and modern transportation networks hurtle the busy inhabitants from place to place.

Tokyo – Japan's capital

Tokyo is the capital of Japan and the seat of its government. It is also the main centre of business, broadcasting, art and fashion in Japan. The city stands in the heart of the Kanto Plain, facing Tokyo Bay on the Pacific coast. More than 8 million people live within the city limits, but the suburbs sprawl over the plain to merge with the port of Yokohama and other towns. Altogether, Greater Tokyo has a population of 26.4 million people and is the largest city in the world.

The capital began life as a tiny fishing village called Edo (meaning 'gate of the inlet') on the banks of the Sumida-gawa River. Edo lay at a junction of important trading routes, and in the 1400s, a lord built a castle here to guard this important point.

東京

The Japanese write the name of their capital with two kanji. The first kanji (tō) means 'east' while the second (kyō) means 'capital'. Tokyo lies on Japan's east coast.

This woodcut shows 19th-century Edo – later Tokyo – a busy city of wooden houses and broad streets.

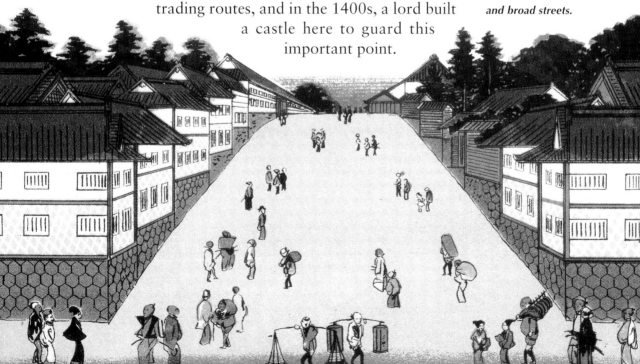

CENTRAL TOKYO

The city of Tokyo is divided into 23 wards, called *ku* in Japanese. Within the wards are many smaller, traditional areas such as Ginza and Ueno.

Through the crowded, bustling cityscape of office buildings, museums, department stores and temples, and across rivers, canals and docks, runs the overhead road network known as the Shuto Expressway. Today, the expressway's 30 sections exceed 220 kilometres (136 miles) in length and in parts is as high as 40 metres (130 feet). The expressway carries more than 1 million vehicles a day.

SHIBUYA-KU

Meiji-jingū Inner Garden

Tenru-ji Temple

SHUTO

SHIBUYA

EBISU

SHUTO EXPRESSWAY

HIRŌ

Shinjuku-Gyoen Garden

National Noh Theatre

Meiji-jingū Outer Garden

HARAJUKU

EXPRESSWAY

AOYAMA

Aoyama Cemetery

SHINJUKU-KU

National Theatre

MINATO-KU

National Diet Building

Imperial Palace

Imperial Gardens

National Museum of Modern Art

Science Museum

CHIYODA-KU

GINZA

Idemitsu Museum of Art

EXPRESSWAY

SHUTO

Tsukiji market

Tokyo Station

EXPRESSWAY

TOKYO PORT

Tokyo Stock Exchange

CHŪŌ-KU

SHUTO EXPRESSWAY

BUNKYO-KU

Kanda-gawa River

EXPRESSWAY

N

Tokyo National Museum

National Science Museum

National Museum of Western Art

Ueno Park

Ueno Zoo

TAITŌ-KU

UENO

SHUTO EXPRESSWAY

ASAKUSA

Sensō-ji Temple

Sumida-gawa

SHUTO

Sumo stadium

Edo-Tokyo Museum

SUMIDA-KU

SHUTO EXPRESSWAY

TOKYO UNDERGROUND RAILWAY

Map labels:
Oji, Sungamo, Ikebukuro, Nishi-Nippori, Kita-Senju, Ayase, Nerima, Korakuen, Ueno, Asakusa, Ogikubo, Nakano, Shinjuku, Suidōbashi, Asakusabashi, Nakano-Sakaue, Iidabashi, Ichigaya, Ogawa-Machi, Akihabara, Motoyawata, Nishi-Funabashi, Yotsuya, Kudanashita, Kanda, Shinjukusanchōme, Nagatacho, Higashi Nihombashi, Aoyamaitchōme, Otemachi, Kokkagijidō-mae, Mitsuko-shimae, Akasakmitsuke, Tōkyo, Ningyocho, Shibuya, Harakucho, Hibiya, Nihombashi, Omotesando, Tameike-sannō, Kayabacho, Ebisu, Kasumigaseki, Ginza, Hatchōbori, Gotanda, Mita, Higashi-Ginza, Shin-Kiba, Shimbashi, Shinagawa

Legend:
- Ginza
- Marunouchi
- Hibiya
- Tozai
- Chiyoda
- Yurakucho
- Teio
- Hanzomon
- Toei Asakusa
- Toei Mita
- Namboku
- Toei Shinjuku
- - - East Japan Railway
- Junction

In 1590, Tokugawa Ieyasu, a powerful warlord, took over the castle and rebuilt it. When he became **shogun** (supreme general of Japan) in 1603, Edo became the centre of the nation's government. During the 17th century, the Tokugawa family continued to rule Japan from Edo.

By the 18th century, Edo was home to 1 million people and was probably the largest city in the world. Apart from their roofs, the houses and even important buildings were made out of wood, making them vulnerable to devastating fires.

In the 19th century, the power of the shoguns passed back to the emperor. In 1868, Emperor Meiji moved his capital from the city of Kyōto to Tokyo. The castle became the emperor's palace. Because Tokyo lay on Japan's east coast, its full official name became Tokyo-to, meaning 'east capital prefecture'. This name is used for administrative purposes and for postal addresses. Usually, however, the name is shortened to Tokyo.

Throughout its history, Tokyo has been ravaged by war and disaster. In 1657, fires gutted nearly half the

Tokyo's underground railway system may look complicated, but in fact it is the simplest way of getting around the city.

35

city. Nearly three centuries later, in 1923, much of the capital was destroyed in the Great Kanto Earthquake (see page 62). During World War Two (1939–45), Allied bombing flattened Tokyo. Both times new buildings rose from the ruins. The result is a mainly modern city, with only a few old buildings. Overhead expressways tower over ancient narrow streets, and shiny skyscrapers dwarf tiny traditional houses and shops.

In Tokyo, as in most of Japan's lowland areas, space is cramped. There are few parks in the city centre. In Tokyo Bay, whole new districts have been reclaimed from the sea for factories and gardens. Every weekday, tens of thousands of office workers surge into Tokyo's city centre. During rush hour, the streets are jammed with cars. The underground trains are so packed that officials called 'pushers' are employed to cram as many people as possible on each train.

Housing is also cramped and very expensive. Visiting business people sometimes sleep in capsule hotels, where each tiny room is the size of a large locker, with space only for a bed, TV and radio.

There is much to see in Tokyo, but foreigners often find it difficult to get around. Few streets have names,

A fast-changing city

Throughout its history, Tokyo has been rebuilt many times – whether because of earthquake, fire or war. Even today – when Japan is peaceful and buildings are built to be earthquake-proof – the cityscape is constantly changing. One of Japan's most famous architects, Toyo Ito, has written: 'Today in Tokyo buildings are constructed and demolished at a bewildering speed. It is really stunning.

Buildings invade the city and gain popularity, then, just as quickly, they are used up and discarded like a piece of paper.' In the 1980s and early 1990s, Japan was so rich that business corporations could afford to put up buildings almost as if they were pasting up an advertisement.

The new buildings display an astonishing variety of styles. In the busy shopping area of Shibuya, there is the rocket-like Humax Pavilion, where young people come to shop and meet friends. In Shibuya, too, is the beautiful new National Noh Theatre, where performances of Japan's ancient theatre take place in a stately atmosphere. Overlooking the Sumida-gawa River is the apartment block pictured here, curving like a white flame. The most spectacular structure in Tokyo, though, isn't a building at all but the vast network of overhead roads that fly over the busy cityscape – the Shuto Expressway (see page 34).

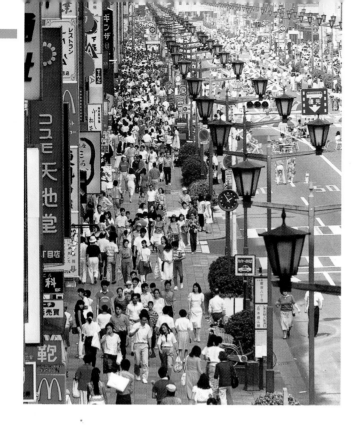

and houses are not numbered systematically. If tourists do get lost, there are special yellow tourist phones that will help them on their way.

The capital is divided into 23 *ku* (wards). Each of these districts is like a little town with its own identity. The heart of the city is Chiyoda ward, where the Imperial Palace (see page 12) lies close to the Central Station. The Imperial Palace is home to the emperor and empress of Japan and

Like New York City, Tokyo is a fast-paced, non-stop city. In busy Ginza ward, shoppers throng the street beneath hundreds of shop signs (see also page 87).

their family. The palace stands in its own gardens, surrounded by high walls and a moat. The east palace garden is always open to the public, but the inner gardens can only be visited twice a year, on the emperor's birthday (23 December) and during the New Year's holiday on 2 January.

South of Central Station lies Ginza, Tokyo's famous shopping area. In the late 19th century, its department stores were among the first brick buildings in Japan. South of Ginza is the Tsukiji Fish Market (see page 80), where in the early morning the fish stalls gleam with squid, crabs and other seafood loved by the Japanese.

Ueno is best known for its beautiful park, and it can take a whole day to explore its sights. In early April, the Japanese flock to the park to see the cherry blossoms. The park includes a lake, the oldest zoo in Japan and many shrines and temples, including the Doll Temple. Museums in the park include the Tokyo National Museum, the Museum of Natural Science and the Museum of Western Art.

Asakusa was once Tokyo's entertainment area, where people in a festive mood came to the **kabuki** theatres and tea houses. Today, little remains of the old district, which was largely destroyed during World War Two. The district's heart, Senso-ji Temple, was rebuilt. Inside is an ancient golden statue of the Buddhist goddess of mercy. According to legend, fishermen discovered the statue in the nearby Sumida-gawa River in AD 628.

Shibuya ward is popular with young people. They come to shop in the huge department stores, and often meet friends at the Shibuya Station beside the statue of Hachiko. Hachiko was a dog who waited outside the station every day for his master to come home from work. One day his master died at work, and Hachiko waited in vain. The dog continued to wait loyally for the next ten years until he, too, died.

In the late 19th century, Asakusa was the site of Japan's first cinema theatres.

Kamakura

Visitors to Tokyo who want to escape the hectic pace of life in the city often go to the ancient city of Kamakura for calm. It was the capital of Japan between 1185 and 1333, when the Minamoto clan ruled Japan as shoguns. The city became an important religious centre, and today there are more than 70 temples and shrines there.

The Zen Buddhist temples and their gardens are quiet places, ideal for the meditation that this kind of Buddhism advises (see page 52). The most famous sight is a bronze statue of the Buddha 11 m (36 ft) high. The Great Buddha dates back to the 13th century and weighs almost 850 tonnes (935 tons). According to legend, the statue was made to celebrate the victory of the Minamoto clan over the Taira clan (see page 53).

The **Shinto** shrines are livelier and more imposing places. At one Shinto shrine, students hang up small wooden tablets called *ema*, on which they write out their hopes for success at school. Another shrine is dedicated to the Shinto god of war, Hachiman.

The Dōtomburu-gawa River flows through Ōsaka's lively Minami ward – an entertainment area crowded with restaurants, cinemas and pachinko parlours.

These are the Japanese characters for Ōsaka.

Ōsaka: a city of business

Ōsaka is Japan's third-largest city. For a long time, the city was the country's main trading centre – ships from all over Japan and further afield sailed into Ōsaka Bay and merchants thronged the city streets. Today, Ōsaka is still a busy, thriving city. In 1996, the total revenue from Ōsaka's economic product was higher than the **gross national products** (GNPs) of all but the top eight economies in the world.

Many Ōsakans are very business minded and they work hard. They speak their own gritty, colourful dialect and have rough-and-ready manners that can shock the more refined inhabitants of Kyōto. People greeting each other in the streets often begin by asking '*Mō kari makka?*', meaning 'Are you making any money?'

Ōsaka was heavily bombed during World War Two. Today, its skyline is dominated by concrete and glass skyscrapers and elevated expressways. Seven underground lines and fleets of buses carry the busy Ōsakans around the city. Canals and rivers criss-cross the city, and on hot summer days, visitors and Ōsakans take to boats that cruise the waterways. There are some spectacular modern buildings. The spaceship-like Ōsaka

Dome is home to the local baseball team, and down in the harbour, the aquarium has the world's largest fish-tank, inhabited by two whale sharks.

Visitors usually come to Ōsaka, however, to see its famous castle (*jō*). The original castle was built for the warlord Toyotomi Hideyoshi, who in the 16th century conquered all of Japan. Some 50,000 people laboured for three years to build the stronghold. The streets around Ōsaka-jō Castle were built like a maze, so that an army approaching the castle could easily be ambushed or trapped by the castle's defenders.

After Hideyoshi's death, the head of the rival Tokugawa clan laid siege to the castle and left it in ruins. The castle was later rebuilt, but since then it has been repeatedly destroyed and rebuilt. Today, there is only a concrete reproduction of the castle's eight-storey tower.

Ōsakans are particularly proud of their city's tradition of *bunraku* puppet theatre (see pages 97–8). The city is home to the National Bunraku Theatre, and the most famous *bunraku* playwright, Chikamatsu Monzaemon, wrote plays about the merchants and other inhabitants of the city.

Young people sometimes like to go to Panasonic Square, which has displays of the latest electronic gadgetry. There are lots of virtual-reality games to try out.

Osaka's city centre is divided between the business-dominated Kita ward in the north and the entertainment quarter of Minami.

CENTRAL ŌSAKA

KITA-KU

HANSHIN EXPRESSWAY

City Hall

Ō-gawa River

Panasonic Square

Osaka-jō Castle

Osaka-jō Castle Park

CHUOI-DORI

HANSHIN EXPRESSWAY

NAGAHORI-DORI

Dōtomburu-gawa River

National Bunraku Theatre

MINAMI-KU

N

To harbour and aquarium

Shitenno-ji Temple

Isshin-ji Temple

Municipal Museum of Art

京都

The name 'Kyōto' is written with two kanji – kyō and to – both of which mean 'capital'. Kyōto was Japan's capital city for more than 1000 years.

Kyōto: the 'heart of Japan'

The ancient and beautiful city of Kyōto in central Honshū was home to the emperors of Japan for more than 1000 years. To the Japanese, Kyōto is *Nihon no Furusato*, the 'heart of Japan'. The city has many historic buildings, including 250 Shinto shrines and 1500 Buddhist temples, but there are also modern shops and restaurants, gardens, museums and a zoo.

Kyōto was the capital of Japan from 794 to 1868. The city was built by the emperor Kammu (736–806). He laid out the network of streets following the example of the

CENTRAL KYŌTO

Central Kyōto is contained within a grid of streets. This map shows the major streets (*dōri*) and wards (*ku*) that make up the traditional heart of the city. This grid system makes it easy to navigate. Kyōto addresses are given as the name of the nearest intersection plus their location *agaru* (up) or *sagaru* (down) from the intersection.

IMADEGAWA-DŌRI

Imperial Palace

KAMIGYŌ-KU

River

MARUTAMACHI-DŌRI

TERAMACHIA-DŌRI

KAWARAMACHI-DŌRI

Kamogawa

Nijō-jō Castle

NAKAGYŌ-KU

OIKE-DŌRI

City Hall

Kyōto Museum

KARASUMA-DŌRI

HORIKAWA-DŌRI

PONTOCHŌ

Takashimaya Department Store

SHIJOO-DŌRI

Hankyu Department Store

N

ancient capital of China, Chang'an (modern Xi'an). Throughout the centuries, Japan's most skilful artists flocked to the capital to work for the emperor, and the city blossomed as a centre for arts and crafts. Over the years, parts of the city were destroyed by fire and earthquakes and rebuilt. Unlike so many of Japan's historic cities, Kyōto was not bombed during World War Two.

Kammu also built himself a palace, but the present imperial palace dates mostly from the 19th century. It includes the ceremonial hall where Japan's emperors were once crowned. The buildings are very simple and stand in expanses of dazzling white gravel and clipped green lawns.

The heart of today's city, however, is Nijō-jō Castle, built by the shogun Tokugawa Ieyasu at the beginning of the 17th century. The shoguns were warlords based in Tokyo (Edo) whose power challenged the supremacy of the emperors. Nijō-jō Castle has mighty fortifications, with thick walls and a moat. Inside there are 'nightingale' floors. These were designed so that if anyone – an assassin or a thief – tried to move quietly down the corridors at night, the boards would squeak, or 'sing like a nightingale'.

On the outskirts of central Kyōto are many beautiful temples. The Golden Pavilion Temple stands three storeys high, and each storey has a roof covered with gold leaf. In the nearby Temple of the Peaceful Dragon is a garden with fifteen rocks set into carefully raked white gravel. The Chionin Temple houses the heaviest temple bell in Japan. It takes seventeen monks to ring the bell. Close by, the Heian Shrine has painted red columns and roofs of glazed green tiles. The Temple of Clear Water to the south is built on a hillside. There are fine views of the city from its large wooden veranda.

Kyoto's Nijō-jō Castle has a commanding view of the city. The castle belonged to the shoguns, who ruled from Tokyo. Its massive walls and watch-towers dwarfed the imperial palace – for hundreds of years, the home of Japan's emperors.

広島

The kanji *for Hiroshima mean 'broad island'.*

Hiroshima: city of war and peace

The prosperous city of Hiroshima lies on six sandy islands in the delta of the Ōta-gawa River in south-western Honshū. It was established in the 16th century when a local warlord built a moated castle on the site.

Today, the city is famous less for its sights than for the terrible moment on 6 August 1945 when the US Army Air Force dropped the world's first atomic bomb (see pages 66–7). The blast flattened the city, killing in an instant some 75,000 people. The survivors suffered physical and mental scars, and many inhabitants of Hiroshima continue to suffer from the consequences of the blast.

The Children's Peace Memorial

In the Peace Memorial Park is the Children's Peace Memorial – a bronze statue of a young girl holding aloft a crane. In Japan, the crane is a symbol of happiness and long life. After the war, many children fell sick with leukaemia – a cancer of the blood that, in this instance, was caused by the radiation from the Hiroshima bomb blast. One girl, Sadako, developed leukaemia at age ten. She became convinced that she would get better if she folded 1000 paper cranes. She died having completed 644 cranes. The people of Hiroshima put up a statue in her honour and as a memorial to all the children who died because of the blast. Even today, Japanese schoolchildren make paper cranes in memory of Sadako and send them in boxloads to decorate the monument.

The surviving inhabitants began to rebuild their city in 1950. Many of the streets and buildings are memorials to those who died in the blast. Every year, thousands of visitors come to the city, which has become a powerful symbol for those who believe that nuclear weapons should be banned.

Not all of the city was rebuilt. Close to the spot where the bomb exploded are the ruins of the Industrial Promotion Hall. The building – now called the Atomic Bomb Memorial Dome – has been left as it was found after the blast. Across the river is the Peace Memorial Park, laid out in 1955 as a place to pray for peace. In the park is a saddle-shaped cenotaph. Beneath the cenotaph is a stone chest in which there is a scroll listing the names of all those who died in the blast. There is also a perpetual flame. When the last nuclear weapon on Earth has been destroyed, the flame will be put out. The park also holds the Children's Peace Memorial (see box opposite).

Nearby is the Peace Memorial Museum, which tells the harrowing story of the blast and its aftermath. Its exhibits include the burnt 'shadow' of a person who was incinerated by the intense heat and a model of the city after the blast.

The old castle has also been rebuilt and houses a museum of the city's history. Every year on 6 August, the people of Hiroshima float paper lanterns down the Ōta-gawa River in memory of those who died in the blast.

Central Hiroshima is built on islands in the Ōta-gawa River delta. The monuments to the people who died in the atomic-bomb blast of 1945 are all around the area of the Peace Memorial Park. The main business district lies to the east.

Past and present

'Summer grass
All that remains
Of warriors' dreams.'

Haiku composed by the Japanese poet Basho (1644–94)
on seeing the grave of the warrior Yoshitsune

The Japanese traditionally date the foundation of their nation in 660 BC, when the legendary emperor Jimmu ascended the throne. They believed that Jimmu was a great-great-grandson of the **Shinto** sun goddess, Amaterasu. Today, we know that although the Japanese islands have been inhabited for thousands of years, the country was in fact united as a nation 1000 years after the legendary date – in about 300 AD.

The rulers who united the country later became the Japanese emperors. A single dynastic line links the earliest emperors and empresses with the present emperor, Akihito. For much of Japan's history, however, the emperors have been little more than figureheads. Between the 12th and the 19th centuries, actual power lay in the hands of warlords called **shoguns** and warriors called samurai. Today, the emperor is the head of state of the Japanese **democracy** that was set up after Japan's defeat in World War Two.

Japan's history has been largely shaped by the fact that it is an island nation. Until the mid-20th century, the country suffered no successful foreign invasions. Japanese society and culture, though rooted in those of its overseas neighbour China, developed largely free of outside influence. In the late 19th and 20th centuries, however, Japan turned outwards. It rapidly **industrialized** and became one of the world's great trading nations.

A ferocious samurai whirls his sword at his enemy. For centuries, the powerful warriors known as the samurai held sway over Japanese society.

FACT FILE

● The Japanese emperors are the longest-reigning dynasty of monarchs in the world. The present emperor, Akihito, is 125th in an unbroken line of Japanese rulers that stretches back to the 1st century BC.

● Each time a new emperor comes to the throne, a lucky name is chosen for his reign. The reign of the present emperor, Akihito, is known as the Heisei ('fulfilment of peace') era.

● National Foundation Day is celebrated on 11 February every year. The day marks the anniversary of the accession of the first emperor, Jimmu.

EARLY TIMES

No one knows exactly when human beings first settled in Japan. Most historians agree, however, that the earliest peoples arrived some 30,000 years ago, crossing the land bridges that then connected Japan with Siberia and Korea. Some people may also have arrived in boats from Polynesia. These first peoples were hunter-gatherers who used stone tools and weapons.

The Jōmon and Yayoi

About 20,000 years ago, the world climate grew warmer. The sea level rose and the Sea of Japan was formed, separating the islands of Japan from the mainland of

The Jōmon year

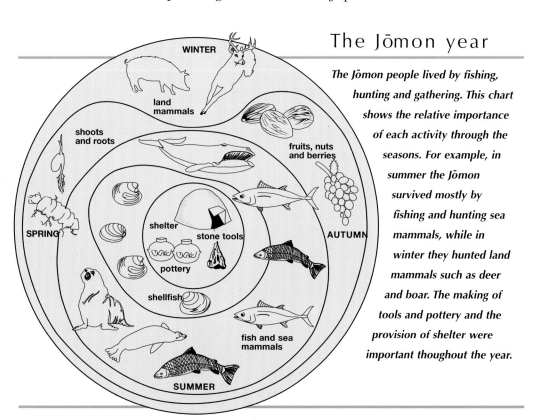

WINTER

land mammals

shoots and roots

fruits, nuts and berries

shelter

stone tools

SPRING

pottery

AUTUMN

shellfish

fish and sea mammals

SUMMER

The Jōmon people lived by fishing, hunting and gathering. This chart shows the relative importance of each activity through the seasons. For example, in summer the Jōmon survived mostly by fishing and hunting sea mammals, while in winter they hunted land mammals such as deer and boar. The making of tools and pottery and the provision of shelter were important thoughout the year.

Asia. The islands grew lusher, and from about 10,000 BC, their inhabitants began to grow vegetables and to fish in the open sea. They also made coiled clay pots, from which their culture gets its modern name – **Jōmon**, meaning 'cord marked'. The Jōmon people wore clothes made from the bark of mulberry trees and wove wicker baskets. They worshipped spirits who inhabited the rivers and mountains of the islands, as well as natural phenomena such as the Sun. These beliefs formed the basis of the Japanese religion known as Shinto (see box).

The Jōmon shared the Japanese islands with another people, the **Ainu**, who originally came from north Asia. Gradually, the Jōmon and their successors drove the Ainu from the fertile lands of Honshū and into cold and inhospitable Hokkaidō (see page 50).

During the Yayoi period (300 BC to AD 300), more settlers reached Kyūshū and western Honshū from China and Korea on the mainland. The newcomers brought new skills: rice-growing, mining, metal-working, weaving and the use of a wheel to make pottery. People lived in settled communities, growing rice and making bronze and iron tools and weapons. Central and western Japan became a patchwork of small, independent states ruled by clan leaders.

Jōmon pots are the world's oldest datable pottery. The Jōmon people used the pots to cook and store food and also buried them with their dead.

Shinto: Japan's native religion

Japan's native religion, Shinto, is very old. It is rooted in the country's landscape and the natural cycle of the seasons. Followers of Shinto worship many spirits (*kami*), the most important of whom is the sun goddess, Amaterasu.

Throughout the Japanese countryside are simple wooden shrines sacred to the *kami*. The shrines have thatched roofs and are entered by way of a painted wooden gateway, known as a *torii*. Worshippers are always careful to purify themselves before approaching the shrine, rinsing their hands and mouth with clean, fresh water. Sometimes, a Shinto priest purifies them by waving a wand of paper strips. Unlike many other religions, Shinto has no holy scripture; instead, its rituals and beliefs have been hallowed by centuries of worship.

The kanji for Shinto – shin and dō – mean 'kami' [gods] and 'way'. Shinto therefore means 'the way of the kami'.

The Ainu: a threatened native people

The Ainu were among the earliest inhabitants of Japan. They are in fact several different peoples, and the word 'Ainu' simply means 'human being' or 'man'. Today, there are fewer than 14,000 Ainu, who live in villages mostly in the Hidaka district, south-east of Sapporo in Hokkaidō.

The Ainu look very similar to the ethnic Japanese but have their own Ainu language. Over the centuries, they have suffered discrimination and today are among the poorest people in Japan. Like other threatened native peoples throughout the world, the Ainu are fighting to preserve their culture.

During the Meiji period (1868–1912), many Ainu customs were banned. Men could not wear earrings, and girls were not allowed to have the traditional blue tattoos around their mouths. The Ainu had to learn to speak and write Japanese. In the 1870s, Ainu people were forced to have Japanese names. When children went to school, they could not study in their own language.

Today, only the Ainu elders remember and recite the old epic poems (*yuka*). These were not written down – people learnt them by listening to others reciting Ainu poetry, song and history. The Ainu and Japanese languages sound quite different. For example, in Ainu 'spring' is '*sak*', while in Japanese it is '*haru*'. Sometimes, Japanese visitors to Hokkaidō find it hard to pronounce Ainu place-names.

In 1997, the Japanese government passed a law that aims to protect Ainu culture for future generations.

THE FIRST EMPERORS

The period of Japanese history between about AD 300 and 710 is known as the Kofun period. The name originates from the great mounds of earth and stone, called *kofun* (literally 'old tombs'), which marked the graves of clan chiefs. Today, the largest known *kofun* is that of the emperor Nintoku, which can be found on the Osaka Plain. The mound is shaped like a keyhole and covers some 200 hectares (500 acres). Originally, the followers of clan leaders were killed and buried with them to serve their leaders in the afterlife. Later, large clay statues of warriors, priests and horses called *haniwa* were put around the mounds.

Soon after AD 300, the head of the Yamato clan from the Osaka Plain became the most powerful chief. Over the next 250 years, the Yamato leaders gradually unified Japan and eventually took the title of *tennō* (literally 'heavenly sovereign'), or emperor. People believed that the emperors were living gods, descended from the goddess Amaterasu. Modern emperors of Japan trace their ancestry back to this clan.

Chinese influence

During the 6th century, the **Buddhist** religion reached Japan from Korea and China, bringing with it a strong Chinese influence. Japanese people adopted many aspects of Chinese culture, including

This haniwa – *clay statue – from the Kantō region is a fully armoured warrior who carries a bow and a sword. The statue is about 1.35 metres (4 feet 5 inches) tall.*

Early imperial Japan was based in the cities of central Honshū.

Early Japan

51

These kanji signify 'Buddha' and 'teaching' and together mean the 'teaching of Buddha' – Buddhism.

its writing system and calendar. From 593 to 622, Prince Shōtoku (574–622) ruled as regent for a young empress. He built many Buddhist temples and adopted Chinese ideas that increased the power of the emperor.

It was Shōtoku, too, who first referred to Japan as the 'Land of the Rising Sun', in a letter to the Chinese emperor. He referred to China as the 'Land of the Setting Sun', implying that he considered Japan to be China's equal. The Japanese people still revere Shōtoku today, and his likeness appears on the 10,000-yen bank note.

The Nara and Heian periods

In 710, the Empress Gemmei founded a new capital at Heijō-kyō, now called Nara. Like Kyōto, the city was modelled on the capital of the Chinese emperors, Chang'an (present-day Xi'an), in a grid-like layout. During this era – called the **Nara period** – Japanese artists created beautiful sculptures of the Buddha, and architects built elegant temples in the Chinese style in which to house them.

Buddhism in Japan

The Buddhist religion developed in India, where its first teacher was Siddhartha Gautama (about 563–483 BC) – the Buddha, or 'enlightened one'. He taught that to achieve happiness, human beings had to suppress their earthly desires. His ideas spread quickly throughout Asia. Different schools, or interpretations, of Buddhism emerged, often as the religion came into contact with different cultures.

Buddhism reached Japan by way of China in the 6th century AD. At this time, Prince Shōtoku built temples and monasteries and wrote studies on Buddhist texts. For this reason, the Japanese consider Shōtoku to be the father of Japanese Buddhism. However, Buddhism did not supplant Japan's native religion, Shinto, and often Shinto and Buddhist shrines stood side by side.

Over the centuries, many kinds of Buddhism have developed. Zen Buddhism emphasizes the importance of meditation in achieving salvation. The Jōdo (Pure Land) school teaches that believers have only to recite a simple prayer to Amida – another name for the Buddha.

As the influence of Buddhism grew, the priests became very powerful. In 794, Emperor Kammu decided to move his capital away from Nara because the priests had too much influence over the court. He built a new capital at Heiankyō, later known as Kyōto (see pages 42–3). The **Heian period**, named after the new capital, was a time of peace and prosperity that lasted nearly 400 years.

During the 9th century, the Japanese broke off relations with China and began to develop their own culture. Japan evolved its own system of writing and produced literature written mainly by women (see page 96). During the Heian period, real power lay not with the emperor but in the hands of a noble family called the Fujiwara. Over the next 300 years, the power of the Fujiwara increased as the clan established large estates throughout western and central Japan.

The rise of the shoguns

The peaceful Heian period ended in the 1160s, when civil war broke out between two rival clans, the Minamoto, also called the Genji, and the Taira. In 1185, the Minamoto family under its chiefs, Yoritomo (1147–1181) and his brother, Yoshitsune, won a sea victory over the Taira. After his triumph, Yoritomo made his capital at Kamakura on the southern coast of Honshū. Jealousy drove Yoshitsune to commit suicide.

Although the imperial capital remained at Kyōto, it was Yoritomo who ruled Japan. In every province there was a military governor called a *shugo*, all of whom reported to Yoritomo in Kamakura. In 1192, the emperor gave Yoritomo the new title of 'shogun', which means 'supreme general'. The rule of the shoguns, called the shogunate in English, continued for nearly 700 years.

The first shogun, Minamoto Yoritomo, was a ruthless and cruel ruler. Later, many plays and stories were written about Yoritomo and his handsome, charming brother, Yoshitsune.

SHOGUNS AND SAMURAI

The period between the 12th and the 16th centuries was troubled and violent, as rival clan chiefs, known as *daimyō*, fought one another to win power. These lords were backed by armies of warriors called samurai (see box opposite). The emperors fought back, rising against the shoguns in 1221 and again in 1333. They failed to regain control of the country, although the shoguns always claimed to govern in the name of the emperor.

The Mongol invasions

At the end of the 13th century, Japan was threatened by a foreign enemy. The great Mongol warlord Kublai Khan (1214–94) had conquered huge swathes of Asia, including China, and founded a mighty empire. In 1274, he launched a naval attack on Japan. Before he could land, however, the weather came to the rescue of the Japanese. The captains of the Khan's troop ships thought that a typhoon was coming and convinced the Mongol leader to withdraw. The Japanese hurriedly fortified their sea defences.

In 1281, Kublai Khan tried again, backed by a huge army of 150,000 soldiers. This time the Mongol fleet landed in Hakata Bay, Kūyshū, and fierce fighting broke out. The Japanese were hopelessly outnumbered. All seemed lost when a sudden typhoon wrecked many of the Khan's ships. The Japanese believed that their prayers for help had been answered and called the typhoon a **kamikaze**, or 'wind of the *kami*' (gods). Heartened, they launched a counter-attack on the Mongols and inflicted massive losses on the invaders.

The Mongol invasions

1 In November 1274, 450 Mongol ships sail from the coast of Korea for Japan. On board are 15,000 Mongol soldiers.

2 In late November, the Mongol ships reach the coast of Kyūshū but almost immediately withdraw.

3 In June 1281, 50,000 Mongols and Koreans and 100,000 Chinese set sail from Korea and southern China.

4 In June 1281, the Mongol fleets land on Kyūshū. For two months the Japanese and Mongols fight in Hakata Bay. Finally, a typhoon wrecks the Mongol ships, and the Japanese inflict heavy losses.

KOREA

Tsushima

Sea of Japan

Honshū

Inland Sea

Hakata Bay   JAPAN

Kyūshū

N

first Mongol invasion
second Mongol invasion

The great Mongol leader Genghis Khan led two invasion forces against Japan from China and Korea. Both attempts were unsuccessful, however. The first foreign occupation of Japan did not occur until the 20th century, after the end of World War Two.

The samurai

The samurai were warriors hired by lords to fight their wars and protect their lands. Expert in fighting with the lance, bow and sword, the samurai swore to defend their master and were expected to die rather than surrender. To avoid disgrace, a samurai warrior committed a kind of ritual suicide properly called *seppuku* or, more commonly, *hara-kiri*. The samurai committing *seppuku* stabbed himself in the stomach, while a servant stood by to strike off his head.

The samurai did no work but were supported by taxes paid to their lord by peasants. The samurai followed a strict code of conduct called *bushidō* ('the way of the warrior'). They were expected to be self-disciplined and loyal. They also had to show generosity and kindness to the poor but had the right to take the life of a social inferior who insulted them.

The privileges and duties of being a samurai were passed from father to son. Gradually, the samurai came to form a separate class, or caste. They also developed a special way of dressing. Only a samurai had the right to carry a sword. He wore his hair tied back in a top-knot and with his brow and crown shaved bare.

When not fighting, a samurai wore simple clothes. In battle, however, samurai wore elaborate suits of armour like those shown here. (The smaller suit was made for presentation to a samurai boy when he came of age at about fourteen.) Samurai rode on horseback and carried a bow and arrows and two swords.

During the peaceful Edo period (1603–1868), the samurai did little to earn their keep. Many samurai became *rōnin*, or warriors without masters, and led a precarious life of duels and daredevilry. The samurai developed their fighting skills into ritual arts, which became the basis for martial arts such as judo and aikido. They also practised kendo (Japanese swordfighting) and *kyudō* (archery). The samurai class was abolished in the late 19th century.

The Age of Civil Wars

In 1336, a samurai lord called Ashikaga Takauji (1304–58) seized power from the Minamoto family and became shogun. The Ashikaga family governed for over 200 years, but the last century of their rule was marked by violence. The period from the mid-15th century to the mid-16th is known as the Age of Civil Wars. The *daimyō* plotted and fought one another to gain land and power, and the central government in Kyōto was too weak to stop them.

Despite all the bloodshed, this was a golden age for arts and crafts. The textiles, ceramics, screen paintings and lacquerware of this time are considered the finest in Japanese history. Many of the practices that are now considered typically Japanese were established at this time, such as **Noh** drama (see page 97), flower-arranging (ikebana) and the tea ceremony (see page 112). Some of Kyōto's most beautiful gardens were laid out at this time (see page 99).

In the late 16th century, two powerful shoguns tried to reunify Japan under their control. Oda Nobunaga (1534–82) was a fierce general and a great patron of the arts. In 1585, Toyotomi Hideyoshi (1536–98) followed in Oda's footsteps. He defeated the other Japanese warlords and even tried to win territory on the Asian mainland. In 1592 and again in 1597, he invaded Korea but was driven back both times.

During the Age of Civil Wars, daimyō families fought each other for supreme power in Japan. The map below shows the various families and their territories.

The civil wars

Uesugi
Hojo
Takeda
Imagawa
Oda
Mori
Otomo

Sea of Japan

Honshū

KYOTO

PACIFIC OCEAN

Kyūshū

N

During the peaceful Edo period, the Japanese nobility enjoyed a life of ease and luxury. At court they wore clothes of gold-embroidered silk, and in their spare time, they practised arts such as calligraphy ('beautiful writing'), landscape gardening and growing miniature trees (bonsai). In this screen painting, aristocrats stroll through the streets of Kyōto, the home city of the Japanese imperial family from 764 to 1868.

THE EDO PERIOD

In 1603, a warlord called Tokugawa Ieyasu (1542–1616) became shogun. Ieyasu was a clever statesman, determined to control all of Japan. He set up his military capital at Edo (now called Tokyo; see pages 33–5), which at this time was little more than a fishing village. Ieyasu set about transforming Edo into a large, busy city. He rebuilt its tumble-down castle, dug canals and laid out roads. He built no defensive walls, but instead relied on numerous blind alleys and gates that were designed to hinder and confuse invaders.

Ieyasu established an orderly and carefully controlled political system. He divided Japan into 250 domains, each ruled by a *daimyō* who had sworn an oath of loyalty to the shogun. The *daimyō* also had to spend a part of the year in Edo. Ieyasu cleverly realized that the *daimyō*

By 1725, Edo had a population of 1.3 million, comprising some 650,000 samurai, 50,000 priests and 600,000 commoners.

'The class of merchants … is very extensive and rich … although their profession is not respected, their wealth is. The commercial spirit of Japan is visible in all the towns and villages.'
Russian visitor to Japan in 1811.

would be far too busy making long journeys to and from Edo to be able to hatch any plots against him. Ieyasu also set up a rigid social hierarchy, with four classes. At the top were the samurai. Below them came the farmers, then the craftsmen and last the merchants or traders. Women were in the same class as their husbands. Strict rules controlled where people in each group lived, the clothes they wore and even the food they ate.

Using this system, the Tokugawa family were able to rule Japan for over 250 years. During their rule, known as the **Edo period**, peace reigned and the cities grew and prospered. The arts, too, flourished. The period saw the birth of **haiku** poetry, **kabuki** drama and woodblock printmaking (see pages 95–8).

The outside world

During the 16th and early 17th centuries, Japan established limited trade and contact with Western nations. The European powers had been interested in Japan since the 13th century when the Venetian traveller Marco Polo (1254–1324) had returned from China with tales of a rich land to the east. In 1543, Portuguese ships reached Japan, bringing with them the first guns that the Japanese had ever seen.

In the early 1600s, the Tokugawas began to fear that trade with foreign countries might lead to invasion by one of the Western nations. The government decided to cut all links with the outside world. New laws decreed that no Japanese could leave Japan and no foreigners could enter.

Christianity in Japan

Soon after the arrival of the first European ships in Japan, the Spanish Catholic priest Francis Xavier (1506–52) landed on Kyūshū and began to preach the Christian faith. Over the next 100 years, Spanish and Portuguese missionaries continued his work and converted thousands of Japanese people.

The Japanese met the new religion with suspicion and sometimes violence. In 1597, for example, 26 foreign priests and Japanese converts were crucified. The persecution of Christians reached a peak in 1637 when the Tokugawas ruthlessly crushed a Christian-led rebellion. Until the end of the 19th century, Japanese Christians had to worship in secret.

Foreign sailors shipwrecked on the coasts were killed, and Western books were banned. During this period of isolation, which lasted over 200 years, the only Europeans permitted to enter Japanese waters were Dutch traders, who were allowed to dock at Nagasaki just once a year.

Japan's policy of isolation was called *sakoku* ('closed country').

Matthew Perry in Japan

By the mid-1800s, the Western countries wanted to renew trade with Japan. In 1853, an American fleet of four ships, under the command of Matthew Perry (1794–1858), sailed into Edo Bay. Perry issued a demand that Japan begin trading with the USA and then sailed away, promising to return the following year. In 1854, the Tokugawa government finally signed a friendship and trade treaty with the USA. Similar agreements with the UK, Holland, Russia and France followed.

The changes helped bring about an end to the rule of the Tokugawa. Soon, powerful warlords were plotting to overthrow the shogunate and restore the emperor to power. They criticized the Tokugawa for the terms of the treaties, which were generally unfavourable to Japan. After the death of Emperor Komei in 1867, the warlords forced the shogun Tokugawa Yoshinobu to resign and made the sixteen-year-old Emperor Meiji head of state. Because the emperor began to rule the country again, this new era was known as the Meiji Restoration.

This woodblock print shows the arrival of Commodore Perry in Edo Harbour in 1853. The appearance of Perry's 'black ship' was a turning point in Japanese history.

IMPERIAL RULE

During the reign of Emperor Meiji (1868–1912), Japan was transformed from a feudal society into a modern industrial nation. The Meiji government looked to the West for inspiration. Japanese leaders were sent to Europe and the USA to learn Western ways, and students went to study at overseas universities. Foreign advisers were invited to Japan to help reform the education and legal systems, transform communications and set up new industries. The Japanese called the new foreign settlers *gai-koku-jin* (literally, 'outside-country-people'). The term is still applied to tourists today in a shortened form – *gaijin*.

In 1889, the first Japanese **constitution** established a parliament of two houses called the Diet (see pages 71–3). The samurai warrior class was abolished and replaced by a modern army and navy. An efficient telegraph system and a railway network were built and modern industries were founded. In the space of less than 50 years, Japan became an advanced, modern country. Backed by a strong army and navy, Japan now set its sights on becoming a powerful force in the Far East.

This woodblock print shows Japan's first railway, which ran from Tokyo to the port of Yokohama. One frequent US visitor to Tokyo was astonished by the changes that the capital had undergone: 'Tokyo is so modernized that I scarcely recognize it ... carriages numerous ... soldiers all uniformed ... new bridges span the canal ... Old Yedo [Edo] has passed away forever.'

Right: These are the kanji *for the Meiji period.*

The growth of the Japanese empire

In 1894, Japan went to war with China over Korea, which both countries wanted to take over. Although China was a much larger country, Japan quickly won the war. The peace treaty with China gave Japan not only some territory in Korea but also the Chinese island of Taiwan.

In 1904, Japan went to war again, this time with Russia, with whom it disputed control of Manchuria, an area in northern China that bordered Russia. Japan wanted Manchuria's rich natural resources, especially its coal and iron ore, for its new industries. The Russian land forces were beaten, and at the Battle of Tsu-shima Island, Admiral Heihachiro Togo sank 35 out of 38 Russian ships. The peace treaty with Russia gave Japan overall control in Korea and southern Manchuria.

At its height in 1942, the Japanese empire stretched from the fog-bound Sakhalin Island in the north to the sun-soaked Pacific islands of the south.

The Japanese empire, 1900–45

Emperor Meiji died in 1912 and was succeeded by Emperor Taisho, who reigned until 1926. Earlier, in 1902, Japan had made an alliance with Britain. When World War One began in 1914, Japan entered the war as Britain's ally against Germany. Japan took the opportunity to seize Germany's Pacific Islands and Germany's holdings on the Shandong Peninsula.

The Great Kanto Earthquake of 1923 virtually flattened the port of Yokohama and much of Tokyo as well. The tremors and fires that followed killed more than 100,000 people and injured another 50,000. Some 3 million homes were destroyed across the Kanto Plain.

The 1920s and 1930s were a very troubled time for Japan. In 1923, the Great Kanto Earthquake devastated the Tokyo region and killed more than 100,000 people.

The worldwide economic **depression** of the early 1930s badly affected Japanese industry. The international price of raw silk – an important Japanese export – fell by two-thirds. Unemployment rose by 3 million, and there was widespread poverty and disease. Nevertheless, this was also a period that saw new business ideas and opportunities. Many Japanese businesses that are now world-famous were set up at this time, including the Toyota and Nissan car corporations and the Fuji film company.

Growing ambitions

During the 1930s, a growing tide of **nationalism** swept Japan. The nationalists – many of whom were soldiers in the Japanese army – believed that the Japanese government was weak and corrupt. They wanted to reassert the traditional values of the samurai – patriotism, loyalty and selflessness – and to stand up to the Western powers.

Many Japanese people supported the army leaders, who believed that Japan needed, and should seize, more territory in order to expand and prosper. In 1931, the Japanese army invaded Manchuria, which had come under Chinese rule in 1907. The Japanese set up a new 'puppet' state called Manchukuo, controlled by Japan. The League of Nations, an international organization that aimed at promoting world peace, condemned the move, and Japan left the league.

Right: These are the kanji for the Shōwa ('radiant peace') period, which began in 1926 when Emperor Hirohito came to the throne.

The nationalist movement continued to gain support. In 1932, nationalists assassinated Japan's prime minister, Tsuyoshi Inukai, because he opposed the army's ambitions. Army leaders gained more and more control over the government. They began to talk of unifying all of eastern Asia under Japanese rule. A year later, Japan went to war with China, and by 1938, Japanese forces occupied a large part of north-eastern China.

The war in the East

At the end of the 1930s, Japan formed alliances with Germany and Italy, both of which were ruled by extreme nationalist dictators. When World War Two broke out in 1939, Japan sided with its allies against Britain and France. In 1940, Japan seized the chance to invade French territories in Indochina – the area between India and China.

In 1941, Hideki Tojo, a general with strong anti-American views, became prime minister. Relations between the USA and Japan became increasingly hostile. The USA banned all exports to Japan, including supplies of oil, iron and steel. Japan hit back, making surprise bombing raids on US military bases in the Pacific, at Pearl Harbor in Hawaii, on Guam and Wake islands and in the Philippines. It was these attacks that brought the USA into World War Two.

During 1941 and early 1942, Japan won dramatic victories. Soon Japanese forces occupied a vast area stretching from Burma and Malaya in the west to the Solomon Islands in the east, and north almost to the Aleutian Islands, which are part of the US state of Alaska.

The Japanese air attack on Pearl Harbor on 7 December 1941 sank or damaged eight US battleships. The USA lost some 2300 men in the attack.

Kamikaze pilots

In 1944, Vice Admiral Takijiro Onishi came up with an extraordinary idea. Japanese pilots were to fly suicide missions, deliberately crashing their planes into US ships to damage and sink them. Onishi realized that it would be difficult to stop the planes because they would have to be destroyed completely before they reached the ships.

The pilots who flew the missions were all volunteers. They became known as kamikaze, meaning 'divine wind', after the typhoon that destroyed the Mongol invasion fleet in 1281.

Before each flight, a kamikaze pilot followed an old samurai custom and tied a special cloth round his head or arm. The cloth was often decorated with an image of the rising sun, a symbol of Japan. Knowing that there was a good chance that they would not come back, the pilots also gave away their personal belongings to friends and wrote farewell letters to their families.

The kamikaze attacks were very destructive, especially as the planes were often packed with explosives. Sometimes two or more planes would crash into a US warship, setting it on fire. In the fighting at Okinawa, a kamikaze force of 1815 planes sank 32 US ships, killing 5000 sailors. Half the Japanese planes were lost.

The tide of war began to turn against Japan in June 1942 when the USA won the Battle of Midway. US experts had succeeded in cracking secret Japanese military codes, and four Japanese aircraft carriers were sunk. By 1945, the USA had begun to bomb factories and cities on the Japanese mainland. Tokyo and other major cities were fire-bombed and nearly burnt to the ground, although the historic city of Kyōto was spared. US forces invaded Japanese territory on the islands of Iwo-jima and Okinawa. Despite the bitter fighting, Japan would not surrender.

To avoid the huge US casualties that would likely result from fighting on the Japanese mainland, the USA decided to use a devastating new weapon, the **atomic bomb**. On 6 August 1945, the first atomic bomb was dropped on the city of Hiroshima. Three days later, another bomb struck Nagasaki (see pages 66–7).

On 14 August, Emperor Hirohito surrendered on behalf of his people. In a radio broadcast, the emperor informed his people of their country's defeat (see box). Japan was forced to accept that it was conquered for the first time in its history.

Surrender and occupation

Under the terms of the surrender, Japan lost all its territories on the Asian mainland and its islands in the Pacific, including Taiwan. Japan's land area was restricted to its four main islands and smaller surrounding islands. The Japanese also had to submit to a military occupation by the Allied forces – mainly US servicemen – under the command of General Douglas MacArthur (1880–1964).

The aim of the Allied occupation was to end Japan's military ambitions and establish democracy. The Allies also wanted to reduce the power of the *zaibatsu*, the large corporations behind Japanese industry that had supported the war. The army, navy and airforce were abolished, and military leaders were tried for war crimes. Some, including former prime minister Hideki Tojo, were executed.

In 1947, a new constitution went into effect, declaring that Japan's sovereignty lay with the Japanese people, not with the emperor. It added that the emperor was not

'Long live the emperor!'

When the voice of Emperor Hirohito was broadcast on the radio at the end of World War Two, it was the first time that most Japanese had ever heard the emperor speak. It was a strange moment for people who believed that the emperor was a god. In fact, some people may not even have understood everything Hirohito said because some words he used were older forms of the Japanese language, used only at the emperor's court.

Since then, much of the mystique surrounding Japan's emperors has disappeared. Nevertheless, today the royal family is still highly respected. As a representative of the nation and a symbol of the unity of the Japanese people, the emperor attends official ceremonies and signs decisions made by the Diet (parliament).

The Hiroshima blast

During World War Two, the US military repeatedly bombarded Japan's cities. In three days of bombing in March 1945, for example, Tokyo was burnt to the ground. More than 100,000 people were killed and thousands more left homeless. By the summer of 1945, hardly a city in Japan was left unscathed.

Remarkably, until August 1945, the city of Hiroshima (see pages 44–5) had not been targeted by the US bombing. On the morning of 6 August 1945, the city's luck changed. At 8:15 a.m., as people made their way to work, the sky above the city erupted into a huge fireball. The US military had dropped the first atomic bomb (A-bomb) used in warfare.

The Americans first developed the A-bomb in 1944–45. The weapon relied on the discovery that when the nucleus of a uranium or plutonium atom is artificially split, a huge explosion of energy – light, heat and radioactivity – is released. The first bomb was tested at a desert site in New Mexico only a few weeks before the Hiroshima explosion.

The Hiroshima bomb – nicknamed 'Little Boy' – had the destructive power of 15,200 tonnes (14,960 tons) of TNT. It exploded 580 m (1900 ft) above the city centre, creating a huge fireball 1 km ($\frac{1}{2}$ mile) in diameter. In a moment, the blast consumed the city – 70,000 buildings and 73,000 people were destroyed in the first few moments. The heat was so fierce that all that remained of some victims were their shadows seared into the rubble.

At the time, the inhabitants of Hiroshima did not know anything about the A-bomb or

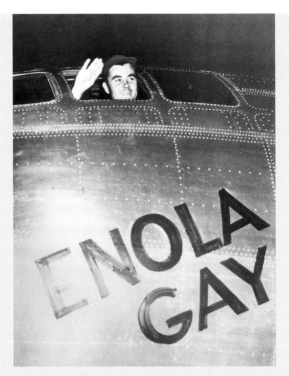

The pilot of the Enola Gay waves from the cockpit on the day of the Hiroshima blast – 6 August 1945.

its devastating power. At first, many thought the city had been struck by ordinary bombs. Only gradually did it become clear that they were the victims of a new and terrifying weapon.

In his famous book about the first A-bomb, *Hiroshima*, US writer John Hersey tells the story of six people who lived through the blast and its aftermath. One woman was at home with her children when the bomb exploded. Hersey reports what happened to her next:

Everything flashed whiter than any white she had ever seen. She did not notice what happened to the man next door; the reflex of a mother set her in motion towards her children. She had taken a single step (the house was 1350 yards [1.2 km] from the centre of the explosion) when something picked her up and she seemed to fly into the next room over the raised sleeping platform, pursued by parts of her house.

Timbers fell around her as she landed, and a shower of tiles pummelled her; everything became dark, for she was buried ... She heard a child cry, 'Mother, help me!' and saw her youngest – Myeko, the five-year-old – buried up to her breast and unable to move. As Mrs Nakamura started frantically to claw her way towards the baby, she could see or hear nothing of her other children.

By the end of 1945, 60,000 more people had died from burns, injuries and radiation sickness. Even today, many people continue to live with the injuries and trauma that resulted both from the Hiroshima blast and from the second bomb blast that devastated Nagasaki. The Japanese call the survivors of the atomic blasts the *hibakusha*.

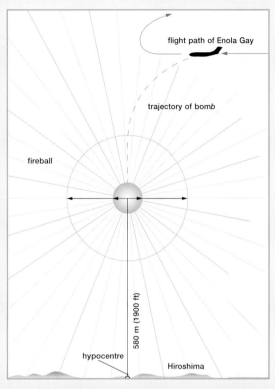

The Hiroshima bomb exploded high above the ground, creating a huge fireball that incinerated the city below. The point on the ground directly below a nuclear explosion is called the hypocentre.

The A-bomb blast virtually flattened the city of Hiroshima for an area with a radius of 2.4 km (1½ miles) from the hypocentre.

67

Altogether, World War Two cost the lives of 1,855,000 Japanese people. Another 678,000 people were either wounded or missing.

a god, as had been previously claimed. Economic and land reforms were also made, aimed at rebuilding Japan's shattered industries and ruined cities.

The Allied occupation was a humiliating blow for Japan, but it did not last long. By 1949, General MacArthur could announce that its main aims had been achieved. When war broke out in Korea in 1950, Japan helped to supply the United Nations (UN) forces with weapons, tools and vehicles. This provided a kickstart for Japanese industry and helped Japan take its first step to becoming an ally of the USA. The Allied occupation ended officially in April 1952, although US forces remained in Japan. In 1956, Japan became a member of the UN.

DEMOCRATIC JAPAN

From the 1950s to the 1970s, there was an 'economic miracle' in Japan. A defeated country, with many of its major industrial centres destroyed, managed to become one of the world's great industrial nations (see pages 75–89) and most stable democracies.

Many reasons lay behind this rapid recovery. The Allies helped Japan to import new technology cheaply, so the country did not need to spend money on research. With no army or navy, Japan spent little money on defence. Factories were rebuilt and the latest equipment was installed. Japan's new industries concentrated on producing goods that would be needed throughout the world. The workers were well trained and highly skilled. They united behind their employers to work long hours, and everyone pulled together to put the country back on its feet.

Japan's car industry was at the heart of the postwar 'economic miracle'. Companies such as Nissan and Toyota led the way in exporting well-built and affordable vehicles around the world. By 1970, Japan was producing more than 3 million cars every year.

68

In 1960, the new prime minister, Hayato Ikeda, announced a national plan that aimed to double the country's income within ten years. The plan was so successful that the average income in Japan doubled only four years later. During the 1960s and 1970s, the country prospered and Japan became a nation of consumers. By 1964, 90 per cent of Japanese homes owned the 'three treasures' – a television, a refrigerator and a washing machine. In the same year, Japan hosted the Olympic Games, which helped establish a new positive image of the country in the world.

The Kuril Islands are a chain of 56 volcanic islands that stretch from Kamchatka to Hokkaidō. Geographically, the islands look like a link between Japan and Russia; politically, however, they have driven the nations apart.

When the Arab–Israeli War of 1973 caused oil prices to rise suddenly around the world, Japanese industry suffered, like that of many developed countries. Japan moved away from heavy industries that relied on fuel and raw materials to concentrate on light industries such as electronics. When the second 'oil shock' came in 1979, Japan was much less affected. In the late 1960s and early 1970s, the USA returned Japan's Pacific island territories, the Bonin and the southern Ryūkyū islands, including Okinawa. The Soviet Union, however, did not return the most southerly of the Kuril Islands – Simushir, Urup, Iturip and Kunasir – near the coast of Hokkaidō, which it had seized at the end of World War Two.

The Kuril Islands

By the 1980s, Japan was the world's third-largest exporter, after the USA and West Germany. Japan invested abroad, opening its first car plants in Sunderland in the UK and in Tennessee in the US. The programme of foreign investment continued in the 1980s, as the value of the Japanese yen continued to rise. By the end of the decade, Japan produced one-third of the world's cars and ships and two-thirds of its electronic goods.

平成

In 1989, Emperor Hirohito died and was succeeded by his son Akihito. This began a new era, known as Heisei, which means 'the fulfilment of peace'. These are the kanji *for Heisei.*

After World War Two, Japan protected its industries by imposing tight controls on **imported** goods, ensuring that Japanese people always bought Japanese products. In the 1970s and 1980s, however, the USA and other countries protested against this system.

Slow down and instability

By the end of the 1980s, the rate of economic growth was slowing in Japan. These new difficulties brought about political change. In 1993, the Liberal Democratic Party, which had been in power since 1955, was defeated, and a new eight-party **coalition** government (a combination of political groups) led by Prime Minister Morihiro Hosokawa took control.

Japan entered a period of instability and uncertainty. Unemployment was on the rise, and the economy was threatened by the collapse of several big banks and companies. To make matters worse, a huge earthquake struck Kōbe in January 1995. The disaster levelled whole districts and killed more than 5000 people. A couple of months later, a religious cult attacked the Tokyo underground with poison gas.

Japan was increasingly criticized by other nations for not playing a more active role in peace-keeping missions around the world. Japan's answer was that its constitution did not allow it to take part in wars, and that it gave huge sums of money in foreign aid. In 1992, however, Japanese troops took part in a UN peace-keeping mission in Cambodia, and Japan agreed to provide UN forces with more support.

The *yakuza*

The *yakuza* are a powerful criminal class in Japan whose influence reaches throughout society, from big business and government to the hospitals and real estate. There are some 90,000 *yakuza* members in Japan, each of whom belongs to one of seven major networks. The largest of these is in Kōbe and has a membership of 20,000. Like the Italian or US mafia, the *yakuza* have a fierce code of honour. A member caught breaking the code is often subjected to violent punishment. Members often have tattoos that cover their whole body. Many Japanese worry that the power of the *yakuza* could undermine democracy.

JAPAN'S GOVERNMENT

Japan is a parliamentary democracy. The emperor is the **ceremonial head of state**, but since 1947, power has been in the hands of the Japanese people. The constitution guarantees its citizens many rights, including freedom of speech and of religion. The proclamation of the constitution is celebrated on 3 May every year with a public holiday.

Voting is considered very important in Japan. Everyone aged twenty and over has the right to vote. Women have had the vote since 1947. On 15 January each year, local town halls hold a civic ceremony to honour those who have reached voting age.

Japan's parliament, called the *Kokkai* (Diet), passes laws and controls taxes. The Diet

The 1947 constitution

The US lawyers who drew up the Japanese constitution of May 1947 modelled it closely on the constitution of the USA. Many of the constitution's articles guarantee fundamental liberties. For instance, one article proclaims: 'All the people should be respected as individuals', thereby abolishing the old legal code that had given husbands unequal rights over their wives. One article, however, is unique and is found in no other constitution in the world: '... the Japanese people forever renounce war as a sovereign right of the nation and the threat or use of force as a means of settling international disputes'.

The National Diet Building – home of Japan's parliament – is in Tokyo, west of the Imperial Palace. The building is modelled on the US Senate Building. To the left is the House of Representatives and to the right is the House of Councillors.

Japan's principal prime ministers since 1945 have been:

Yoshida Shigeru (1946–47 and 1948–54)

Kishi Nobusuke (1957–60)

Ikeda Hayato (1960–64)

Sato Eisaku (1964–72)

Nakasone Yasuhiro (1982–87)

Miyazawa Kiichi (1991–93)

Junichiro Koizumi (2001–)

has two houses. The *Shūgiin* (House of Representatives), the more powerful house, is made up of 500 members, who are elected for four years. The *Sangiin* (House of Councillors) has 252 members, elected for six years. The head of government (prime minister) is chosen by the Diet and is usually the leader of the party with the majority. The prime minister appoints the *Naikaku* (Cabinet) of ministers. In turn, the Cabinet appoints the chief justice and fourteen senior justices who make up the *Saikō Saibansho* (Supreme Court). The government offices are situated in the Kasumigaseki district of Tokyo.

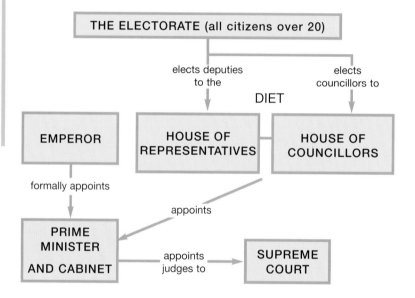

Japan's system of government is like a mixture of the British and US systems. The emperor, like the British king or queen, is the symbolic head of the nation but has no real power. In common with the US system, there are two elected houses, or democratic bodies.

In local government, Japan is divided into 47 administrative units, or prefectures (see page 18). Each prefecture has its own elected governor and assembly. Within each prefecture, each city (*shi*), town (*machi* or *chō*) and village (*mura*) has its own mayor and local assembly.

Parties and elections

Japan has numerous political parties. The most successful, however, is the Liberal Democratic Party (LDP; in Japanese *Jiyu-Minshuto*). This **conservative** party was set up in 1955 and remained in power for nearly 40 years.

THE JAPANESE DIET IN 2002

House of Representatives
500 members • last election 2000 • elections held every four years

Party	%
LDP (Liberal Democratic Party)	48%
DPJ (Democratic Party of Japan)	26%
New Komeito	6%
CPJ (Communist Party)	4%
others	16%

House of Councillors
252 members • last election 2001 • half of members elected every third year for a six-year term

Party	%
LDP (Liberal Democratic Party)	45%
DPJ (Democratic Party of Japan)	24%
New Komeito	9%
CPJ (Communist Party)	8%
others	14%

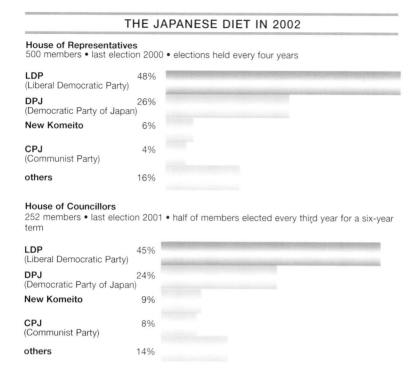

The Liberal Democratic Party remains dominant in both houses of the Japanese Diet. The principal party of opposition is the Democratic Party of Japan. In recent years, however, the New Komeito (Clean Government Party) has gained more and more support.

It is popular in rural areas and with business corporations. Other major political parties include the Democratic Party of Japan (DPJ), the Socialist Democratic Party of Japan (SDPJ), New Komeito and the Japanese Communist Party. Since 1996, the country has been run by a coalition, in which the LDP holds the most seats.

Japanese troops in Cambodia wear the blue beret of the United Nations peace-keeping forces.

The economy

'In all sorts of handicrafts … they are wanting neither proper materials, nor industry and application … they rather exceed all other nations in ingenuity and neatness of workmanship.'

17th-century German visitor to Japan Engelbert Kaempfer

The Japanese economy is one of the strongest in the world. In only 100 years from the 1870s, Japan grew from a poor, undeveloped country into a rich, **industrial nation**. Japan emerged from World War Two defeated and financially ruined. However, during the 1950s and 1960s, Japanese industry shrewdly reinvested profits into research and development. By the mid-1970s, Japan was filing more patents than the USA.

Today, Japan's economic output ranks second in the world – after the USA and followed by Germany. With few **natural resources**, the key to Japan's success is foreign trade. In terms of **exports**, its strength lies in manufacturing. Japanese cars, ships and **consumer goods** are sold all over the world. Almost one-quarter of Japan's workers are employed in manufacturing and construction. Other major industries include services, transportation, farming and fishing.

MAIN ECONOMIC SECTORS

as % of GNP

2 agriculture
39 industry
59 services

source: Government of Japan

THE WORKFORCE

%

6 agriculture
33 industry
61 services

source: Government of Japan

The trading floor at the Tokyo Stock Exchange can be a whirlwind of activity, with traders buying and selling stocks and shares at a frantic pace.

FACT FILE

● In 2000, Japan's **gross national product** (GNP) was second only to that of the USA.

● In Japanese companies, workers are treated equally. Bosses and junior staff wear the same uniform and eat in the same cafeteria.

● Toyota City on Honshū used to be called Koromo. Now it is named after the company that employs 90% of its inhabitants.

● At a Honda factory, a car leaves the assembly line every 43 seconds.

● Four of the top ten largest businesses in the world are Japanese. The other six are American.

MAIN TRADING PARTNERS

EXPORTS

%	
27.2	USA
7.1	South Korea
6.3	Taiwan
6.2	Hong Kong
5.3	China
5.1	Singapore
42.8	others

IMPORTS

%	
22.7	USA
11.6	China
4.6	South Korea
4.4	Indonesia
4.3	Taiwan
4.1	Australia
48.3	others

source: Government of Japan

The vast majority of Japan's trade – both imports and exports – is with the USA. This in part reflects the role played by the USA in the reconstruction of the Japanese economy after World War Two.

TRADE

Japan relies on foreign trade to pay for its **imports** of fuel, raw materials and other products. With around 10 per cent of the world export market, Japan is a major player in international trade. Its most important partner is the USA, which provides Japan with almost one-quarter of its imports, and, in turn, takes about 27 per cent of Japanese exports.

Japan also has important trade links with South-East Asian countries on the shores of the Pacific. Industry in these countries – including Taiwan, South Korea, Singapore, Indonesia and China – is developing fast. Australia, too, is an important trading partner.

Since the 1980s, the value of Japan's exports has exceeded the value of its imports. This results in a net profit known as a **trade surplus**. In the late 1980s and early 1990s, Japan's trade surplus was the largest in the world. This was partly due to the work of the Ministry of International Trade and Industry (MITI), which supports Japanese industries and funds new research. The MITI also protects Japanese trade by restricting imports – limiting the quantity of goods that can enter Japan and imposing taxes on foreign imports.

Japan's import restrictions apply especially to farm products. For example, the price of Japan's homegrown rice is very expensive, but by law, imports of rice are banned. In recent years, nations such as the USA have objected to this arrangement, which places foreign products at a disadvantage. At one point in the 1980s, Japan's trade surplus with the USA was in excess of £19,000 million. Now Japan has agreed to try to reduce its trade surplus by lifting barriers to foreign trade and increasing imports.

MAJOR SECTORS

Japan is one of the most industrial-ized countries in the world. Along the coasts of Honshū and Kyūshū is a dense network of factories, ware-houses and transportation systems.

Small-scale farming

Farms occupy only 12 per cent of the land in Japan. The rest of the country is too mountainous to farm or is occupied by towns and facto-ries. Because space is tight, a typical Japanese farm covers only about 100 hectares (250 acres), which is slightly more than the average of 65 hectares (160 acres) in England. Crop yields in Japan are high because the land is farmed intensively, using fertilizers and weedkillers. Machines do much of the work. Altogether, Japan produces about 70 per cent of its food; the rest is imported.

Before World War Two, most farmland was owned by wealthy landlords. Tenant farmers worked the land, but up to half of their harvest went to the landlords as rent. After the war, the ownership system was reformed, and small farmers were given help to buy land. Now most farmland is owned by the families who work it.

EXPORTS (£000 m)		IMPORTS (£000 m)	
motor vehicles	31.7	mineral fuels	37.9
office machinery	18.3	agric. products	31.8
chemicals	18.0	textiles	16.0
scientific equipment	10.9	chemicals	14.5
iron & steel	9.5	wood	9.0
total (inc. others)	256.8	total (inc. others)	218.2

source: Government of Japan

Since the 1980s, Japan has exported much more than it has imported. The value of its current account balance in 2000 stood at £66,800 million.

This Japanese farmer is harvesting potatoes. Because arable land is so scarce and fragmented in Japan, fields – and the machinery needed to farm them – are often small scale.

Farmers make up only 6 per cent of the Japanese work-force. Most farmers also have full-time jobs in offices or factories and farm only on weekends. National holidays such as Golden Week in early May coincide with busy periods in the farming year, so farmers can spend time in the fields, planting or harvesting.

Many young people from farming families do not wish to work on the land. Instead, they leave country areas to seek better-paid and less back-breaking work in towns and cities. Today, most farmers in Japan are older people, aged 55 and over.

LAND USE

Japan's mountainous inland is densely forested. Crop lands are confined to narrow coastal strips.

crop land

forest

pasture land

Rice is by far the most important crop in Japan. It is the staple food and is eaten at nearly every meal. All over Japan, steep, hilly land is cut into steps to make flat terraces that can be planted with crops or flooded to make paddyfields for rice. In the past, the island of Kyūshū in the south was the main rice-growing region. Now, hardier strains of rice have been developed, and most rice is grown in Hokkaidō in the north.

Rice amounts to one-third of Japan's total harvest. Other important crops are wheat, barley, tea and tobacco. Vegetables and fruits include sweet potatoes, aubergines, sugar beet, radishes, carrots, cabbages, watermelons, strawberries and tomatoes. Apples and pears are grown in the north, while southern orchards yield tropical fruits such as mandarin oranges, peaches, tangerines and nectarines.

The island of Hokkaidō is one of the least developed parts of Japan and is an important farming area. The main crops grown here are oats and potatoes. Beef and dairy cattle are raised on grassy pastures. The lowlands around the shores of the Inland Sea in the south of Japan yield many kinds of fruit. On the southern coasts of Kyūshū and Shikoku, the main crop is sweet potatoes.

Traditionally, few animals were reared for meat in Japan because it is against **Buddhist** principles to kill animals. Today, meat has become much more popular. Chickens are reared for eggs and meat and pigs are raised for pork. Cattle are reared for beef and dairy products. Beef from cattle raised near the city of Kōbe is an expensive delicacy. The cattle are kept underground, fed on beer and massaged every day.

Forests cover 67 per cent of Japan, but the country harvests little of its own timber. Wood is imported from the tropical rainforests of South-East Asia, which have suffered huge environmental damage as a consequence. Nevertheless, there is growing awareness and concern about the logging of the tropical rainforests in Japan, as in other parts of the world.

A great fishing nation

Traditionally, fish forms a main part of the Japanese diet. It is eaten either raw, grilled or fried. Fishing is a major industry in Japan. The country's fishing fleet is the largest in the world, with more than 400,000 fishing vessels. The fleet cruises the waters of the Indian, Pacific and Atlantic oceans, and also visits the icy seas of the

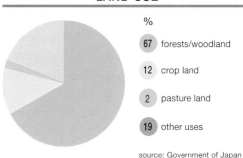

LAND USE

%

67   forests/woodland

12   crop land

2   pasture land

19   other uses

source: Government of Japan

This chart shows the percentages of land given over to various uses.

Silk farming

Central Honshū is famous for its mulberry trees. The leaves are used to feed the larvae (young) of silkworm moths, which are raised on special farms. From its saliva, each silkworm produces silk to make a cocoon, a kind of case that protects it while it changes from a caterpillar into an adult moth. The cocoons are unwound and spun into a thread, which is then woven into silk fabric. Since a cocoon weighs approximately 8 decigrams (0.02 oz), it takes thousands of cocoons to make 1 kg (2.2 lb) of raw silk. As a material, silk is soft, strong and warm in cold weather. Japanese silkworms produce 40,000 tonnes (39,400 tons) of silk each year.

Potential buyers inspect frozen tuna during an auction at the Tsukiji Fish Market in Tokyo.

Arctic and Antarctic in search of good fishing grounds. Tuna, salmon, pollock and squid are some of the most important catches. In open waters, fishing boats net cod and sardines. Closer to shore, mackerel and shellfish, such as crabs, shrimps and clams, are caught. Each year, Japan nets over 12 million tonnes (11.8 million tons) of fish – one-eighth of the world's catch.

Environmentalists criticize Japan for its practice of drift net fishing. Two boats drag a fine net between them, sweeping up everything that lies in their way. The net is usually about 15 metres (50 feet) deep and the two boats hauling it can be as much as 50 kilometres (30 miles) apart. The fishermen are aiming to catch tuna, but turtles, dolphins, sharks and countless other sea creatures get caught up in the nets too and are left to die.

In the past, Japan was an important whaling nation. Today, there is an international ban on whaling, though Japanese ships continue to catch some whales for what the Japanese say are 'scientific purposes'.

Fish is the major source of protein in the Japanese diet. On average, each person in Japan eats 30 kg (66 lb) of fish every year.

Many different kinds of fish are farmed in Japan. Carp, trout and eels are reared inland in ponds and tanks. Tuna and sea bream are farmed in sheltered coastal bays. Seaweed is also harvested on the coasts around Japan for use in cooking.

Natural resources

Japan's economic success is all the more remarkable because its natural resources are very limited. Its mines produce copper, lead, limestone, manganese, tin, zinc, gold and silver, but not in quantities large enough to meet the country's needs. Most of the minerals and metal ores necessary for industry, including large amounts of copper and bauxite, are imported.

Large quantities of iron and coal are used by Japan's iron and steel industry. The country imports iron ore from Australia, Brazil and India. Japan has coal mines on Hokkaidō and Kyūshū, but they produce only low-grade coal that is expensive to mine. To supply its industries, Japan imports large stocks of coal from Australia, Canada and the USA.

With only poor-grade coal, Japan lacks the rich deposits of fossil fuels – formed from the remains of animals and plants – needed to meet its energy needs. The main fuel used for generating energy is oil, but the small deposits of oil found on the north-west coast of Honshū meet only a tiny fraction of the country's needs. Once again, Japan must import supplies. Oil comes mainly from the Middle East, but also from South-East Asia, Mexico and China. Crude oil, together with natural gas, represents a large percentage of the total value of all the goods and raw materials that Japan imports from overseas – some 17 per cent in 1996.

Some of Japan's energy needs are met by the nuclear power and hydroelectricity generated by the country's fast-flowing rivers. Japan has more than 40 nuclear power stations (see box).

ENERGY SOURCES

%
55.2 oil and petroleum products
16.4 coal
12.3 nuclear
11.3 natural gas
3.4 hydroelectricity
1.4 other

source: Government of Japan

Japan depends on fossil fuels such as oil, coal and gas to meet its energy needs.

Nuclear power

Japan's decision to build nuclear power stations was made despite protests from many Japanese people. The Japanese have been sensitive to the dangers of nuclear radiation ever since the USA dropped atomic bombs on Hiroshima and Nagasaki during World War Two. In 1999, moreover, a nuclear explosion at a uranium-processing plant north-east of Tokyo injured nineteen workers. In the future, Japan may rely more on renewable energy sources, such as wind power and geothermal energy.

81

A wealth of manufacturing

Today, almost every home in developed countries contains Japanese products. But the success of Japan's manufacturing industry dates back only 50 years. At the end of World War Two, Japan's factories lay in ruins. The Ministry of International Trade and Industry (MITI) rebuilt factories and encouraged exports.

The steelmaking and shipbuilding industries were the first to be redeveloped in the 1950s. Then came the consumer industries, producing goods such as cameras and cars. In the 1970s, Japan switched to lighter industries such as electronics, which relied less on imported materials and more on skilled workers. Recently, new industries such as aerospace and biotechnology have also become important.

The success of Japanese manufacturing lies in good management, company loyalty and hard work. Japanese firms invest large sums in developing new products. Their factories use the latest equipment and technology, including robots.

Today, the most important industries in Japan are the car industry and electronics. Iron, steel and shipbuilding are still important, as is the petrochemical industry, which refines oil and makes plastics. Japan is also world-famous for making precision equipment, such as binoculars, watches and musical instruments, and for cement, textiles, clothing and ceramics.

The main manufacturing region in Japan lies on the southern coast of Honshū, from the western tip of the island east as far as Tokyo. All along the Pacific coast, factories

These women are working on a production line making televisions in a factory near Ōsaka. Sony, Mitsubishi and Toshiba are world-famous brands of electrical equipment and have pioneered new developments, such as flat-screen TVs and the PlayStation.

MAJOR INDUSTRIES

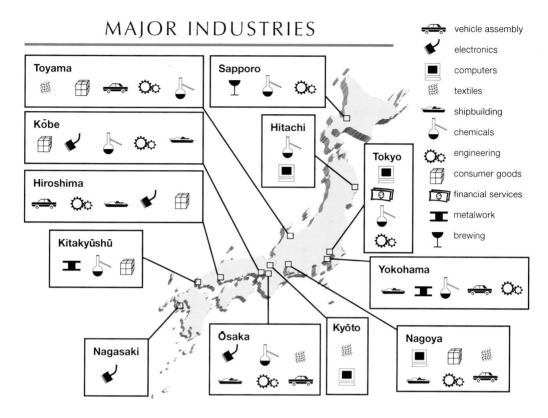

Legend:
- vehicle assembly
- electronics
- computers
- textiles
- shipbuilding
- chemicals
- engineering
- consumer goods
- financial services
- metalwork
- brewing

Toyama: textiles, consumer goods, vehicle assembly, engineering, chemicals

Sapporo: brewing, chemicals, engineering

Kōbe: consumer goods, electronics, chemicals, engineering, shipbuilding

Hitachi: chemicals, computers

Tokyo: computers, financial services, chemicals, engineering

Hiroshima: vehicle assembly, engineering, shipbuilding, electronics, consumer goods

Kitakyūshū: metalwork, chemicals, consumer goods

Yokohama: shipbuilding, metalwork, chemicals, vehicle assembly, engineering

Nagasaki: electronics

Ōsaka: electronics, chemicals, textiles, shipbuilding, engineering, vehicle assembly

Kyōto: textiles, computers

Nagoya: computers, consumer goods, textiles, shipbuilding, engineering, vehicle assembly

have grown up around ports that receive vital supplies of fuel and raw materials. The regions around Tokyo and Nagoya are known for vehicles, machinery and chemicals. Ōsaka and Kōbe produce machinery, iron, steel and chemicals. Kōbe is famous for its shipyards.

Further west, in the lowlands around the Inland Sea, including northern Shikoku, vehicles, ships, iron and steel are produced. The Hokuriku region on the west coast of Honshū is famous for textiles and chemicals. Western Kyūshū produces cars and electronic goods.

Japan's iron and steel industries were redeveloped after World War Two. The steel is used to make ships, cars, machinery and buildings. Along the Pacific coast, some iron and steel plants have been built on land reclaimed from the sea. The shipbuilding industry also developed from knowledge and skills acquired in wartime. The shipyards sprang up near steel mills because they used large quantities of steel. In the 1960s and 1970s,

Most of Japan's industry is found on Honshū island, especially in the Tokyo and Ōsaka regions.

Japanese factories are some of the world's most advanced. Production lines such as this one are monitored by computers and are highly efficient.

Japan built the first supertankers and supplied over half of the world's ships. Today, the industry is less important but still builds 40 per cent of the world's ships.

Japan's vehicle industry is the largest in the world. With nearly 28 per cent of the world market, it outstrips even the USA. When the first Japanese cars reached Western countries in the 1960s, they were not considered serious competition. Now Japanese firms produce 8 million cars and 7.5 million lorries and buses each year. More than half these vehicles are exported to Europe and North America. The motor industry employs more than 5 million workers in Japan alone; giant companies such as Mitsubishi, Honda, Toyota and Nissan employ thousands more in factories worldwide.

The electrical and electronics industry has mainly developed since the 1970s. Now Japanese radios, stereo systems, television sets, video recorders, DVD players, calculators, fax machines, cameras and computers are popular all over the world. Japan produces most of the world's industrial robots used in factories and 80 per cent of all microchips – the tiny circuits that run electronic equipment. In the early years of the industry, Japan imported technology from the USA and Europe and used it to develop highly successful products. More recently, products such as the video recorder and the personal stereo were invented in Japan. Now companies are focusing on digital technology, lasers and fibre optics as well as electronics.

Industrial pollution

Japan's rapid industrial growth from the 1950s has been achieved at the expense of the environment. Factories belched smoke, soot, sulphur and nitrogen dioxide into the air. Exhaust fumes from cars added lead and toxic gases such as carbon monoxide. By the 1970s, air pollution in some cities was so bad that people had to wear face masks.

Factories also discharged poisonous chemicals such as mercury and cadmium into streams and rivers, polluting water. Between 1956 and 1967, one chemical company discharged waste containing mercury into Minamata Bay in Kyūshū, poisoning the local fish and shellfish. People who ate seafood from the bay became very ill. Up to 20,000 people were affected by 'Minamata Disease' and 857 later died. Many suffered severe damage to the nervous system. In the 1970s, people living near Toruku Mine on Kyūshū were poisoned after their drinking water was polluted by arsenic from the mine.

Today, Japan's government imposes strict anti-pollution controls on factories. Cars run on unleaded petrol and are fitted with catalytic converters to reduce toxic exhaust gases. The air, land and water in Japan are now much cleaner than they were twenty years ago.

In many areas, national parks have been established to protect the environment. Japan also has a good record of recycling materials such as glass and paper.

Working life

Work dominates life in Japan far more than it does in many developed countries. Most people work six days a week and take only one or two weeks' holiday each year.

In offices and factories, the day begins with workers bowing to each other and singing the company song. Everyone joins in physical exercises before meeting to discuss the day's work. Employees work late and are expected to go out and socialize with co-workers after work. Ambitious executives do not get home much before midnight, and Sunday is the only day when people spend time with their families. Recently, people have begun to recognize the dangers of overwork. After a number of exhausted businessmen dropped dead in the street, the Japanese invented a term for the phenomenon – *karōshi*, meaning 'death by overwork'.

Unemployment in Japan has traditionally been very low. More recently, however, levels have increased. Among young adults, about 6 per cent are unemployed.

These Japanese office workers are exercising together before beginning the day's work. Team spirit is very important in Japanese companies. Wearing the same clothes and eating together are thought to improve productivity and create a close-knit community.

Most visitors to Japan come from the neighbouring countries of South Korea and Taiwan.

MAIN OVERSEAS ARRIVALS

%

- 26 South Korea
- 18 Taiwan
- 14 USA
- 6 China
- 36 others

source: Government of Japan

Almost a third of all Japanese workers work for a big company. Employees traditionally join when they leave school and stay with the same company until they retire. There are very few strikes. Employers expect hard work and loyalty. In return, the company provides employees with cheap housing in a suburb near the factory. It pays for health care, arranges annual holidays and even provides scholarships for workers' children. This system, called lifetime employment, is still common in big companies, though recently some firms have been hit by economic difficulties and have had to dismiss personnel.

TRANSPORTATION

Japan's transportation system is extremely efficient. Plans are underway to develop networks of new motorways, **bullet trains** and airports so that any part of Japan can be reached from Tokyo in under 90 minutes.

The rail network

Japan's rail network is fast and efficient. It was begun during the Meiji Restoration in the 1870s. Now trains carry 40 per cent of travellers in Japan. The Japan Railways Group is the biggest railway operator.

In the 1960s, Japan pioneered high-speed trains. Today's *shinkansen* (bullet trains) are among the fastest in the world. These services run from Morioka in northern Honshū to Fukuoka in Kyūshū in the west, travelling at speeds of up to 275 kilometres (170 miles) per hour. Some fast trains are double-deckers. When trains pull into main stations, passengers are already waiting in line on marks painted on the platform. These show the position of the doors of the trains, which always stop in the same spot.

Japan's largest cities all have underground railways. During rush hour, the trains are very crowded. Shinjuku Station in Tokyo is one of the busiest in the world. Trains arrive every minute, and officials called *oshiya* (literally, 'pushers') stand by to help cram commuters on trains.

In the 1990s, a new kind of train was being developed in Japan. Maglev – an abbreviation of 'magnetic levitation' – trains will travel at speeds of up to 480 kilometres (300 miles) per hour. Magnets on the underside of the train and on the track repel each other, causing the train to float above the track.

Japan's first underground railway system was built in 1927 in central Tokyo. Today, there are also underground systems in Ōsaka, Nagoya, Sapporo, Yokohama, Kōbe, Fukuoka and Kyōto.

A bullet train crosses a bridge in Ginza, one of Tokyo's busiest districts.

As in the UK, cars in Japan are driven on the left side of the road.

Busy roads

Japan has over 1 million kilometres (620,000 miles) of roads. Most roads run north to south, using the flatter ground near the coasts, rather than west to east across the mountains. Motorways link all the major cities. There are more than 30 million cars in Japan and more than 20 million lorries. Most freight goes by road, but driving is not a very efficient way for passengers to travel in Japan. Fuel is expensive and the roads are very congested. During rush hour, the traffic jams around Tokyo may stretch for 80 kilometres (50 miles) or more. Special boxes by the roadside provide drivers with the latest satellite information about congested routes. Parking in large cities has become a major problem. To register a car, drivers must first prove they have somewhere to park it.

Over the last twenty years, a vast network of bridges and tunnels has been built to carry road and rail traffic between Japan's four main islands. In 1998, the longest suspension bridge in the world – the Akashi Kaikyō Bridge – opened, helping link Honshū and Shikoku.

In Kōbe's busy, smoky harbour, industrial wharves, docks and industrial plants are built on land reclaimed from the sea.

TRANSPORTATION

Japan has a well-organized and highly efficient transportation system. More than 20,000 kilometres (12,400 miles) of railway track link Hokkaidō with Kyūshū. Air travel is cheap and there are numerous ferry services to Japan's many islands.

——— major roads

+++++ railways

✈ major airports

HOKKAIDŌ

Asahikawa
Otaru
Sapporo
Kushiro
Hakodate
Chitose
Muroran
Seikan Tunnel
Aomori

HONSHŪ

Akita
Morioka
Yamagata
Sendai
Niigata
Kōriyama
Iwaki
Kanazawa
Toyama
Kōbe
Tottori
Tokyo
Yokohama
Chiba
Kammon Bridge and tunnels
Hiroshima
Shimonoseki
Kyōto
Okayama
Nagoya
Ōsaka
Kitakyūshū
Fukuoka
Ōita
Kōchi
Seto–Chuo Expressway
Nagasaki
Naruto
Kōbe–Awaji Naruto Expressway (including Akashi Kaikyō Bridge)
KYŪSHŪ
Matsuyama
Kurume
SHIKOKU
Kagoshima

Air and water

Flying is the quickest way to travel in Japan. There are 70 local airports. Japan is the only country that uses jumbo jets for internal flights because so many people want to travel by air. There are several international airports; Tokyo has two – Haneda and Narita. Most international flights land at Narita, which is located 60 kilometres (37 miles) north of the city. An efficient train link – the Narita Express – runs between Tokyo and Narita Airport. More airports are being built on artificial islands constructed along the Pacific coast to serve the largest cities.

In the past, people used ferries to travel between Japanese islands, but today ferries are used mainly to link the smaller islands. The country's merchant fleet is the third largest in the world. Japan's main ports – Chiba, Kōbe, Nagoya and Yokohama – all lie on the east coast of Honshū.

The Tokyo–Chitose (Hokkaidō) air route is the busiest in the world. Six million passengers fly this route every year.

Arts and living

'Japan is a country that permits the harmonious existence of old and new. Japan's very existence and functioning have been built upon this harmony.'

Japanese sociologist Kato Hidetoshi

Many of the things today considered typically Japanese have their origin in China. The ornate Japanese script, elegant silk clothes, refined literature and **Buddhist** religion were all borrowed from the court of the Chinese emperors in about the 6th century. During the **Heian period** (AD 794–1185), however, Japan shook off the influence of China and began to build a rich and original culture that was all its own.

For centuries after, Japan was virtually a closed world. The traditional culture that developed was very formal. Elaborate rules governed everything from greeting acquaintances to writing poetry. Tradition and refinement were valued more highly than originality or self-expression. People thought of themselves less as individuals than as part of a society in which rules and duties were to be followed for the greater good.

Then, in the mid-19th century, Japan opened itself to the outside world. Its people enthusiastically adopted the technologies that came from the West – films, trains and factory machines – and in many cases, improved on them. Japanese culture nevertheless modernized without losing any of its originality. Today, life in Japan is an often astonishing mix of the traditional and modern. Japanese cities blend red-and-gold temples with daring modern skyscrapers, and Japanese homes are likely to have both a state-of-the art computer and an abacus.

Japanese arts often have a spiritual quality. Rock ('flat') gardens such as this one at Tōfuku-ji Temple in Kyōto are designed to encourage meditation.

FACT FILE

- Japanese people do not wear shoes inside their homes. They leave their shoes outside and wear plastic slippers inside.

- 85% of Japanese couples marry in a **Shinto** ceremony.

- The Japanese population is the longest-living in the world. On average, people in Japan live to 81.5 years of age.

- In 1999, the Japanese spent £6196 million on books. Only the USA spent more.

- According to the United Nations (UN) Human Development Index, the Japanese people have the ninth-best quality of life in the world. The UK ranks tenth.

THE ARTS

A succession of trips to China by envoys and students during the ancient period (AD 250–710) and the **Nara period** (AD 710–784) meant that early Japanese arts were influenced by those of China. Today, many traditional crafts also have the status of art forms. Activities as diverse as garden design, paper-folding, writing, flower-arranging and even drinking tea are all 'arts' in Japan and often have a spiritual dimension.

Architecture old and new

In Japanese cities, ancient and modern often exist side by side. Here the gabled curving roofs of Ōsaka Castle contrast with the shiny twin office buildings behind.

Many of Japan's most beautiful buildings are its Buddhist temples and **Shinto** shrines. The earliest shrines were simply sacred places – a grove, rock or pool, for example – that were separated from the surrounding land by a rope. Later, the shrines became simple wooden-framed structures guarded by a *torii* – a gate with two uprights and two cross-pieces. The main path to the shrine is often flanked by stone lion-like creatures called *komainu*.

Because Buddhism came to Japan by way of China, traditional Buddhist temples were influenced by Chinese architecture. They have slender pillars and are painted in bright colours such as red and gold. Their tiled roofs have edges that sweep upwards in pleasing curves. The temple often features a tower-like **pagoda** (see page 99), which houses a relic – a tooth or bone, for example – of the Buddha.

Some modern Japanese architects echo the graceful lines of traditional architecture in new buildings. Kenzo Tange, one of Japan's most popular architects, designed the National Stadium in Tokyo and the Peace Centre

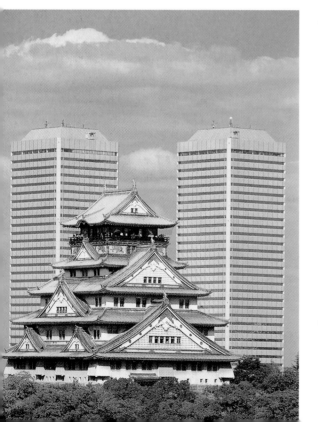

in Hiroshima. Traditional Japanese architecture has also influenced architects worldwide. For example, Robie House in Chicago, built by American architect Frank Lloyd Wright (1867–1959), has Japanese-style long, low balconies and roofs.

Buildings in Japan are sturdily constructed to withstand the shocks of small earthquakes that shake the country daily. Traditional houses are made of wood, a material flexible enough to bend with minor tremors. In cities, skyscrapers are built of steel and concrete but are also designed to sway in earthquakes, rather than topple and collapse. Most Japanese homes are small, and rooms are created with movable partitions, or screens, that can be slid to one side to make living spaces larger or smaller.

Buddhist temples are built around a central compound and consist of several buildings.

Sculpture: *haniwa* and *netsuke*

The earliest-known sculptures are the clay statues known as *haniwa* that date from the Kofun period (AD 300–710). *Haniwa* are simple figures of warriors, servants and animals that were placed in the burial mounds of chieftains to honour or serve the lord (see page 51).

After Buddhism reached Japan in the 6th century, sculptors produced works for Buddhist temples using wood, clay or bronze. One of the most famous is the Great Buddha of Kamakura, a giant bronze figure cast in the 13th century. Statues of Buddha or Buddhist priests had calm faces. Other figures, such as the Guardian Kings at Kamakura, are carved with ferocious, threatening faces to frighten away the enemies of Buddha.

At the other end of the scale from these massive sculptures are the tiny sculpted figures known as *netsuke* that date back to the 17th century. They are carved in minute detail in wood or ivory and were designed to be attached to a bag or a medicine box by a silken sash.

The main parts of a Buddhist temple are:

kondō or hondō: the main halls of the temple where the statues of the Buddha are placed
pagoda: a tiered, tower-like building that houses a relic of the Buddha
kōdō: the lecture hall where the monks study and recite scriptures
chūmon: the inner temple gate, often guarded by fierce-looking stone figures.

Hokusai: 'the old man mad about drawing'

One of the very greatest woodblock artists was Katsushika Hokusai (1760–1849). Hokusai lived almost all his life in Edo (Tokyo), where he began his career as a book illustrator.

In 1814, he began work on a series of *manga* (cartoon) sketchbooks in which he drew the bustling street life of Edo. In the *manga* is everyone from acrobats and musicians to geishas and samurai.

Later in life, Hokusai turned his hand to producing bold, colourful views of Japan's beautiful landscapes. His most famous series of prints depicts Japan's holiest place – Mount Fuji. In his *Thirty-six Views of Mount Fuji*, Hokusai depicted its snow-capped cone from many vantage points (see page 21). In the *Great Wave at Kanagawa*, the holy mountain is just visible in the trough of a giant breaking wave.

Hokusai produced an enormous amount of work – more than 30,000 prints, sketches and paintings. He signed his work with many different signatures – changing his name more than 50 times. Hokusai appeared frequently among his names, but his favourite, adopted late in life, was a name meaning 'old man mad about drawing'.

Painting: 'images of the floating world'

Early Japanese painting was also inspired by Buddhism and influenced by China. Between the 12th and 14th centuries, artists painted long picture scrolls that told the stories of heroic battles or ancient legends through a series of images that were 'read' from right to left. Other artists painted wooden screens or drew witty caricatures – pictures that distort a person's features – that portrayed noblemen and officials as monkeys, frogs and other animals.

From the 14th century, many artists influenced by the **Zen** school of Buddhism produced peaceful landscapes in ink wash (diluted ink powder). In the 17th century, coloured woodblock prints became fashionable. The artist drew the original picture on transparent paper, which was then stuck onto a piece of cherrywood. The engraver then cut out the wood through the paper to make a woodblock for printing. A woodblock was cut for each colour that had to be printed; sometimes up to ten separate blocks were used. Two famous woodblock artists were Andō Hiroshige (1797–1858) and Katsushika Hokusai (see box opposite).

Woodblock prints were cheap enough to be bought and enjoyed by ordinary people. They showed fleeting impressions of landscapes, beautiful women or scenes from plays or legends. The woodblock tradition is called *ukiyo-e*, which means 'images from the floating world'. In the 19th century, the prints reached Europe, where they were much admired by artists such as Édouard Manet, Mary Cassatt and Henri de Toulouse-Lautrec, who imitated their bold compositions and flat, pure colours in their own work.

The Japanese woodblock artists of the Edo period produced striking images of the natural world. This painting of a white heron landing on a pond edged by violet irises is by Andō Hiroshige – one of Japan's greatest artists.

Haiku

Haiku poems express brief and meaningful insights into nature or human life in seventeen syllables. The pioneer of the form was the poet Matsuo Basho (1644–94). An artist as well as a poet, he travelled around Japan, visiting some of his country's more remote regions and composing poems about his impressions of the sights he saw.

The mood of many haiku is often thoughtful, but there can be moments of humour, too. Another poet, Kobayashi Issa (1763–1827), wrote the following well-known haiku:

For fleas, also, the night
Must be so very long,
So very lonely.

Slowly, slowly, climb
Up and up Mount Fuji
O snail.

Some translations of haiku poems may have more than the required seventeen syllables because it is not always possible to give the meaning in another language in only seventeen syllables.

Novels and haiku

One of the earliest and most important works of Japanese literature is a long novel called *The Tale of Genji*. It was written in the early 11th century by a lady at the imperial court, Murasaki Shikibu (*c*.978–1014). Her novel tells of the travels and adventures of young Prince Genji. It was written in Japanese at a time when the language of the court was Chinese and only women and ordinary people spoke Japanese. Lady Murasaki also kept a diary, which gives intimate descriptions of life at the imperial court.

Lady Murasaki's novel contains lots of poetry – a favourite pursuit of the aristocracy of the period. Lady Murasaki would probably have known the *Manyoshu*, the first collection of Japanese poetry, compiled in about 750. The *Manyoshu* includes about 4500 poems written mostly during the 7th and 8th centuries.

One of best-known forms of Japanese poetry is the **haiku** (see box). In Japanese, there must be five syllables in the first line, seven in the second and five in the third, making a total of seventeen syllables. Another traditional form is the *tanka*, which contains 31 syllables. Today, there are poetry clubs in many Japanese towns and cities where members practise writing haiku or *tanka*.

Japan also produced many fine novelists in the 20th century. One of the most talented, Mishima Yukio (1925–1970), committed suicide in the manner of the samurai to protest against the Westernization of Japan.

In traditional Japanese puppet theatre – bunraku – the puppeteers make little attempt to hide themselves. They move the puppets so convincingly, however, that the audience is drawn into the play and almost forgets that the puppeteers are there.

Traditional drama

Japanese theatre has many traditional forms. **Noh** theatre dates back to the 14th century. More than half the plays performed today were written by Zeami Motokiyo (1363–1443), his son or his grandson. The plays proceed at a solemn and stately pace, with music and dancing. Actors wearing carved wooden masks take the roles of heroes or villains and act out stories from history or legend. Many of the lines are chanted by a chorus.

Often more than one Noh play was performed at a sitting. In between these serious plays, maskless actors performed a kind of farce known as *kyōgen* to provide a light-hearted break for the audience.

Another form of theatre, **kabuki**, first developed in the 17th century. The actors wear bold make-up and bright costumes and act in a lively, exaggerated style. Kabuki plots are dramatic tales of love, jealousy, loyalty and revenge. The audience is swept along in the action, cheering the heroes and hissing at the villains. Kabuki is thought to have originated from the dances that a shrine

The word 'kabuki' is made up of three Japanese characters: 'song' (*ka*), 'dance' (*bu*) and 'skill' (*ki*).

Many of Japan's traditional instruments derived from those played in neighbouring China and Korea. The biwa, for example, was introduced from China in the 7th century.

maiden from Izumo shrine, named Okuni, performed to raise money. Nevertheless, women are not allowed to act in Noh or kabuki plays, so the female parts are played by men.

Bunraku, or puppet theatre, dates from the same time as kabuki. A narrator tells the story and puppets act out the plot. The largest puppets, which are two-thirds life-size, are operated by three puppeteers at once. The puppeteers dress in black and are hidden from the waist down by a screen. The puppet master, who has often trained for as long as 30 years, operates the puppet's head and right arm. Many of the best *bunraku* plays were written by Chikamatsu Monzaemon (1653–1724), often regarded as Japan's equivalent to English dramatist William Shakespeare.

Music traditional and new

Many of the instruments and forms of traditional Japanese music were introduced from China in early times. At the emperor's court, small orchestras played a refined music called *gagaku*. Music often accompanied performances of *bunraku* and kabuki theatre. During Buddhist and Shinto ceremonies, priests chanted or struck bells and drums.

Traditional instruments include the three-stringed *shamisen*, which has a long, unfretted neck and a rectangular or circular soundbox. The flat, thirteen-string *koto* is laid on the ground to be played with a pick and sounds like a harp. Another string instrument is the lute-like *biwa*. Flutes, drums and gongs are also played. The *shakuhachi*, a bamboo flute, has a breathy, haunting sound. *Taiko* drumming is another traditional Japanese music that is still popular today at festivals and parades. The drums are very large, and the drummer needs lots of energy.

Today, Western music forms are popular in Japan, including classical, rock, jazz and pop. There are seven concert orchestras, based in Tokyo, Ōsaka and Kyōto.

shō (mouth organ)

shamisen

biwa

Garden design

Japan is celebrated for its **landscape gardening.** Unlike European and American gardens, Japanese gardens rarely feature grass lawns or flowers. Instead, they are a meticulous arrangement of rocks, streams, trees, bushes or sand, composed just like a painter composes colour and shapes on a canvas. Even the landscape outside the garden plays a part in the composition of a Japanese garden – perhaps a distant mountain or a temple pagoda.

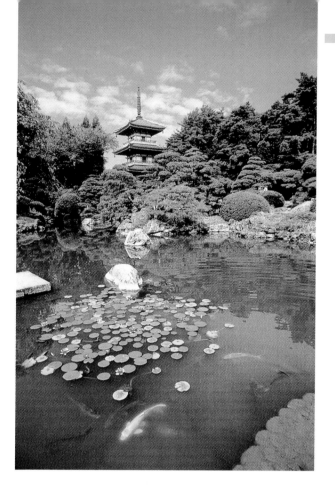

There are three main kinds of gardens. Tea gardens are created around tea houses (see page 112). The trees and bushes of the tea garden are carefully clipped into shape. A path of stepping stones is laid through the garden, and there is a stone basin for guests arriving at the tea ceremony to wash their hands. At night, the flickering light from a stone lantern adds to the atmosphere of peace and intimacy.

Hill gardens, mostly designed for private homes, are small parks with well-planned displays of flowering shrubs and small, artificial hills. The Jojuin Gardens at Kiyomizudera in Kyōto and Ritsurin Garden in Kumamoto, Kyūshū, are two of the best-known examples.

Flat gardens are quiet places for meditation, designed according to the principles of Zen Buddhism. They have few plants but feature flat areas of sand or gravel carefully raked into patterns around rocks or pools that represent mountains, rivers and oceans. The most famous flat garden is in Ryoan-ji Temple in Kyōto.

Japan's temples often stand in beautiful and tranquil gardens. They are places in which to stroll and meditate. This garden is at Rinno-ji Temple in Sendai, northern Honshū. The temple's pagoda rises above the well-tended shrubs and bushes, while carp swim in the peaceful pond. The Japanese associate the carp with strength and determination.

Exquisite crafts

Japan is famous for the beauty of its ceramics, silks, embroidery, lacquer and cloisonné (decorative enamelling). Lacquer are items such as bowls, trays and boxes that are skilfully painted with lacquer, a varnish made from tree sap. Up to 50 steps are involved in lacquering even a simple bowl. Japan's fine metalwork, including armour, swords and knives, has been renowned from ancient times.

Japan is also well known for its handmade patterned papers (*washi*). During the Heian period, people at court used *washi* to write poetry. Sometimes special papers were made to complement the style of a particular poem. Other traditional crafts, such as **origami** (paper-folding), ikebana (flower-arranging) and calligraphy (the art of beautiful writing with a brush pen) are popular leisure activities. Origami models are made by folding coloured paper into shapes that can be as complicated as a flower. A favourite is to make an origami crane, which is a symbol of long life (see page 44).

There are more than twenty different styles of arranging flowers. In fact, ikebana does not always feature many flowers. It is more likely to be a careful arrangement of branches and leaves, positioned according to a set of rules. The finished arrangement represents Heaven, Earth and humankind. An upward-pointing branch represents Heaven, one leaning to the right stands for humankind and one leaning to the left indicates the Earth.

This intricate lacquer box was made in the 19th century and was used to hold gloves.

The film industry

Japan is a leading filmmaking nation. In the 1950s, films featuring a monster called Godzilla, which were directed by Honda Ishiro (1911–93), achieved cult status in Europe and the USA because of their special effects. A popular kind of film in Japan was the adventure story dealing with the samurai. The *Seven Samurai*, a 1954 film by Kurosawa Akira (1910–98), was later remade as the Hollywood western *The Magnificent Seven*

Motion pictures were first shown in Japan in 1896. The first Japanese film was made in 1899.

(1960). Another Kurosawa film, *Yojimbo* (1961), became *A Fistful of Dollars* (1964), starring Clint Eastwood. Kurosawa's film *Ran* (1985) was his version of Shakespeare's play *King Lear*.

One of the greatest Japanese filmmakers was Ozu Yasujiro (1903–63). Starting as an assistant cameraman at the age of twenty, he went on to direct 54 films. Most of them were shot in a simple style from a low viewpoint, as if the camera was held by someone sitting on a traditional *tatami*-mat floor. This meant that Ozu had to take the unusual step of building ceilings on film sets because they often appeared in shots. The films, which include his masterpiece, *Tokyo Story* (1953), tell the stories of the lives and problems of ordinary Japanese families.

Japanese animated films are also popular. One well-known film, *Akira* (1987), by Otomo Katsuhiro, is based on *manga*, Japanese adult comic books that are often criticized for their violent content.

Two generations of a Japanese family sit down to drink tea and chat. The Japanese rarely use chairs but sit on cushions on the floor.

EVERYDAY LIFE

Family life in Japan has been transformed in the last hundred years. A century ago, the vast majority of people lived in the countryside. Eldest sons typically followed their father's profession. Families were often large, with grandparents, parents and their children, and sometimes uncles and their families, all living together under one roof. Most married couples had four children or more. Marriages were arranged by the couple's parents, helped by a matchmaker. When the eldest son married, his wife came to live with his family. Wives worked in the home almost like servants and obeyed their husbands in all things.

How to say ...

The Japanese language can seem very odd to English speakers (and vice versa). For example, Japanese has no words for 'the' or 'a', and there are no plural forms of nouns (you may have noticed that in this book words like 'haiku' or 'samurai' are spelt just the same whether there are one or many poems or warriors). Lots of Japanese words, too, are pronounced the same but have different meanings – for example, 'hashi' can mean both 'chopsticks' and 'bridge'. What is more, Japanese is written with a system of characters, or **kanji**, which can look bewildering to Western eyes (see page 108).

The Japanese are very polite. Co-workers address each other not by their first names but by their family names, followed by '-san', which can stand for 'Mr', 'Mrs', 'Ms' or 'Miss'. Even friends use each other's surnames, but adding '-chan' for girls and saying '-kun' instead of '-san'. Japanese are especially courteous to people older than themselves or to those who hold a more senior position – at work, for example.

Despite such difficulties, it is not hard to learn how to say some simple Japanese phrases. A few are written below using the Roman alphabet, together with a rough pronunciation guide. The vowels written with a bar (macron) are pronounced just the same as standard vowels but are held twice as long. A lengthened vowel can make all the difference to the meaning of a word. For example, while 'yuki' (without the macron) means 'snow', 'yūki'(with the macron) means 'bravery'.

Please (when asking for something)
   o-negai shimasu (o-nengi she-
   ma-su)
Please (when offering something) *dōzo*
   (doo-zo)
Thank you *domō arigatō* (do-mohh
   ah-reeng-ah-tohh)
Yes *hai* (hi)   No *iie* (i-eh)
Good morning *o-hayō gozaimasu*
   (o-ha-yohh go-zigh-ma-su)
Good afternoon *konnichiwa*
   (kon-nee-chee-wa)
Good evening *kombanwa*
   (kom-ban-wa)
Goodbye *sayōnara* (sigh-yohh-na-la)

How are you? *o-genki desuka?*
   (oh-gen-kee deh-su-ka)
Sorry *gomen nasai* (go-men na-sigh)

Numbers:
One *ichi* (ee-chee)
Two *ni* (nee)
Three *san* (san)
Four *yon* (yon)
Five *go* (go)
Six *roku* (lo-ku)
Seven *nana* (na-na)
Eight *hachi* (ha-chee)
Nine *ku* (ku)
Ten *jū* (juhh)

Bowing

In Japan, people bow to greet one another or when apologizing. Bowing (*ojigi*) takes the place of the Western custom of shaking hands.

It takes a long time to master the art of bowing. Mothers teach babies how to bow, and children continue to learn the rules of bowing at school. New company employees also spend time during their first weeks learning how to bow at work.

The depth of bow depends on the status of the person you are greeting. People bow at 15° to greet equals, a little further forward at 30° to superiors and a deep bow at 45° to apologize or greet very important people. The habit of bowing becomes so automatic that many people bow when speaking on the telephone. Many younger Japanese no longer bow and prefer to shake hands in formal situations, especially with foreigners.

These days, things are very different. Most sons now choose their own careers. The majority of people live in the city, where space inside houses is too cramped for grandparents to live with their relatives. Family units are much smaller: often just a mother and father and one or two children. Marriages are no longer arranged, so people marry for love and shared interests. More married women now go out to work, though not usually when their children are young. On average, men marry aged about 28 and women at about 25.

The Japanese at home

Japanese homes are small. The floors are covered with springy straw matting called *tatami*. No one wears shoes inside the house. People leave their outdoor shoes at the entrance and put on slippers instead. In the home, life goes on at ground level. Everyone sits on cushions on the floor. In winter, people warm themselves by sitting around a low table covered with quilts, with a heater underneath. At night, padded mattresses called futons are spread out on the floor for bedding. By day, the futons are packed away in cupboards so that the same room can double as a bedroom and living space.

The Japanese have used the metric system of measurement for decades. However, they still measure rooms in terms of the number of *tatami* (straw mats) that they will hold.

The Japanese have some of the best-equipped homes in the world. Almost all Japanese homes have a colour television, washing machine and refrigerator.

WHAT DO THE JAPANESE OWN?

99.2% televisions
100% telephones
83.1% cars
99.3% washing machines
98.1% refrigerators
25.2% computers

source: Government of Japan

Most Japanese homes have many modern appliances, including a colour television with cable and satellite channels, video recorder, stereo system, computer and fax machine. There may be at least one Western-style room with a carpet, chairs and a higher table. The main room of the house always has a traditional feature – a wall niche with a decorative scroll and flower arrangement. In the evenings, people often enjoy a relaxing soak in a deep bath. They soap and rinse before getting in the tub because they sometimes share the same hot water.

Clothes – 'things worn'

In everyday life, Western-style dress is very common. Business people wear suits and leather shoes to work. At home and for informal occasions, most people wear casual clothes such as jeans or tracksuits and trainers. Most city people are more fashion conscious than those in country areas.

Traditional clothes are usually kept for special occasions. The **kimono** ('thing worn'), the traditional dress for both men and women, is a long, loose garment tied at the waist with a sash called an *obi*. Wooden clogs called *geta* or flat sandals called *zori* are worn on the feet. There are special socks called *tabi* to wear with the V-shaped straps of the *geta* or *zori*. These are something like mittens for feet, with a section for the big toe split from the larger section for the other toes.

This elaborate embroidered coat was intended for wearing at court. The traditional clothes of today are usually much simpler.

104

Girls and women wear kimonos for visiting shrines (see page 111) and at coming-of-age ceremonies, graduations, weddings and funerals. Boys and men can also wear kimonos for ceremonial occasions but these are often in darker colours – blue or brown.

Uniforms play an important part in daily life. People working in department stores, factories and offices in some large companies wear uniforms.

Food and drink

Rice is a staple food for Japanese people. In fact, the Japanese word for 'rice' also means 'a meal'. Rice is eaten at every meal and is usually boiled. It is also made into cakes, moulded into cubes and patties and even used to make the rice wine known as sake. Fish is the main form of protein. It is prepared in many different ways: grilled, deep-fried in batter with vegetables as tempura or eaten raw. Several kinds of seaweed are eaten, too.

Sashimi are thin strips of raw fish. Sushi are rice patties seasoned with vinegar and topped with raw fish, seaweed or vegetables. People sometimes dip the sashimi or sushi into a mixture of soy sauce and wasabi, a spicy radish paste, before eating them. Small pieces of pickled ginger also add to the flavour.

A chef puts the finishing touches to an elaborate dish. Japanese food is not only delicious, it is also beautiful to look at. The finest kind of Japanese food is known as kaiseki and is made from only vegetables and fish.

People traditionally ate little meat in Japan because it was against Buddhist principles, but times have changed. Meat is much more popular today, along with bread and dairy products. Sukiyaki is a dish made with thin slices of beef and chopped-up vegetables, all simmered in a soy and sake sauce.

Soya beans are another rich source of protein. Salty soy sauce is used to flavour food. Soya beans are also fermented and ground to make miso paste for soup or

105

Japanese green tea

You can make Japanese green tea easily at home. A widely available green tea is called *bancha*, which is also very cheap. Boil 850 ml (1½ pints) of water. Put 2 tablespoons of green tealeaves into a pot. When the water has boiled, carefully pour it over the tealeaves and leave it to steep for about two minutes.

Pour the tea into cups through a strainer. Don't add milk or sugar, as these will spoil the tea's delicate flavour.

In summer, the Japanese like to drink green tea cold. First, they roast the green tealeaves in a pan for a few minutes, which gives the tea a delicious smoky flavour. Then they make the tea in the normal way, straining it and keeping it in the refrigerator.

made into blocks of curd called tofu. A filling winter dish called *oden* contains grilled and fried tofu, fish, cabbage, carrots and other vegetables. Tea is the most popular drink. Alcoholic drinks include beer and sake.

Breakfast is a full meal, consisting of boiled rice, dried fish, seaweed, miso soup and pickles. These days, some people prefer a Western-style breakfast of cereal, toast and coffee. The midday meal is often a box lunch (*bento*) containing rice, raw fish and a little meat, pickle and tofu. The evening meal consists of a wide variety of dishes, all served at the same time.

The Japanese version of fast food is noodles, made of different kinds of flour. *Soba*, made from buckwheat flour, are brown; *udon* are made from white flour. Noodles are often served in broth, with vegetables, shrimps, egg or meat added. In summer, noodles are eaten chilled and topped with dried seaweed and a dipping sauce. When people are eating in a noodle bar, there may sometimes be some loud slurping noises. It is not considered rude, just a way of showing you are enjoying the food. In hamburger restaurants, there are the usual burgers and some special dishes for Japan, such as teriyaki burgers flavoured with soy sauce and octopus salad.

Japanese sweets are very different from the sugar-based kind found in the West. They are often made from a sweet red-bean paste called *anko* and thick, sticky rice.

It is common to take guests out to eat at a restaurant rather than invite them home for dinner. Most restaurants serve only one kind of food, such as sushi or noodles. The presentation of each dish is very important – the food must be carefully arranged to look its very best and most appetizing (see page 105).

One very unusual Japanese food item is the bony fish known as *fugu*, or puffer. It is a popular delicacy in restaurants. *Fugu* chefs are specially trained to remove all the parts of the fish that are poisonous. Each year, however, people still die from eating *fugu* that has not been correctly prepared.

Education

Schooling starts early in Japan. Many children attend play school from the age of three. Formal schooling begins at six and is compulsory and free until the age of fifteen. Pupils spend six years at primary school, followed by three years at junior secondary school. Most students then go on to study at a senior secondary school for another three years to prepare for university or college training. There are more than 450 universities in Japan and about 600 colleges.

Japanese children work very hard at school. Monday to Friday, school hours are 8:30 a.m. to 3:30 p.m. Children also go to school on Saturday mornings. At primary and junior secondary school, a lot of time is spent learning to read and write the difficult Japanese language (see page 108). Many junior and senior secondary school students study English, too.

Throughout their school career, students face examinations. Some children take their first exam at three to get into the best play schools. Students must then pass exams each year. The entrance exams for colleges and universities are very difficult. Many pupils go to *juku* (cramming schools) for extra classes that will help them to pass these exams. No wonder that this time of a student's life is known as 'examination hell'.

EDUCATIONAL ATTENDANCE

further (university; 18+)	21.2%
secondary (13–18)	96%
primary (6–12)	100%

The chart above shows the percentage of Japanese who study at each stage of education.

Learning Japanese

Japanese is a complicated language that takes many years to learn to write. It has three different scripts. The most important is the *kanji* script, which takes its name from the characters called *kanji.* It is used to convey basic words such as nouns and verbs.

 If you look at the *kanji* for rain (left), for example, you can almost see rain streaming from a rain cloud. Originally, *kanji* came from China, but over the years they changed their forms and the Japanese invented new ones.

Simple *kanji* were used to build more complex ones. The *kanji* for 'forest' (right), for example, is made up of the *kanji* for 'tree' repeated three times. Similarly, the *kanji* for 'plum tree' (left) also contains the *kanji* for 'tree'. Japanese schoolchildren learn nearly 2000 different *kanji*.

Another script, *hiragana*, is used to show the grammatical endings of words. A third script, *katakana*, which has 46 letters, is used for writing foreign words. Many foreign words are written using *katakana* – for example, *bijinesuman* (businessman) and *gorufu* (golf). Some borrowed words sound so different in Japanese that they are hard to recognize. If foreign words are too long, Japanese shorten them – for example, *waapuro* (word processor).

A healthy nation

In Japan, people expect to live to an old age. The average life expectancy – 78 for men and 85 for women – is the highest in the world. This long life is partly due to the healthy Japanese diet.

The standard of health care is also high. Hospitals and doctors' offices use the latest medical equipment and there is good health education in schools and among the public. Health care is paid for by medical insurance. Sixty per cent of this insurance is provided by private businesses, which cover the costs of their employees' treatment. Private medical insurance pays for the rest. Most doctors and hospitals in Japan use Western type medicine, but oriental medical techniques are also practised.

Japan has 16.5 hospital beds per 1000 people in the population – the second highest number in the world after Switzerland. The UK has 4.2.

Sport and leisure

Many different sports are played in Japan. One of the most popular is baseball, which was introduced from the USA in the late 19th century. Japanese baseball is called *yakyū*. *Yakyū* has different rules from the US game and is played on a smaller field. There are two national leagues – the Central and Pacific leagues. League games are shown on television in summer, and most people follow the progress of their favourite team.

Sumo (Japanese wrestling) is the national sport and probably the oldest sport in Japan. It began in the 3rd century AD and the first contests were held at Shinto shrines. The referees still dress as Shinto priests. Sumo wrestlers, called *rikishi*, are large and powerful, some weighing more than 150 kilograms (330 pounds).

Each year, some 800 wrestlers take part in eight tournaments. Tickets for the tournaments sell out quickly, and the contests are also shown on television. Champion wrestlers are rich and famous. A skilled wrestler named Chiyonofuji recently held the title of Grand Champion for ten years.

Sumo bouts take place in a circular ring called a dohyo. The loser is the first man to step outside the ring or touch the ground with any part of his body except his feet. The referee, dressed in ceremonial Shinto robes, makes sure the rules are followed.

HOW THE JAPANESE SPEND THEIR MONEY

%

24.3 food/drink/tobacco

20.5 transport/ communications

10 entertainment/sports

6.2 housing

5.5 clothing

3.5 health/medicine

30 other

source: Government of Japan

The Japanese spend most of their income on food and transport.

The Japanese love music. In 2000, they spent £32 per head on CDs, tapes and records. The UK spent £30 per head.

Japan is well known for its martial arts. Most school-children – girls as well as boys – learn at least one form of self-defence. These ancient sports developed from the fighting skills of samurai warriors. Practice begins with silent meditation to help focus the mind. Judo, meaning 'the way of gentleness', aikido, meaning 'the way of spiritual harmony', and karate, meaning 'empty hand', are all forms of unarmed combat. The traditional art of archery is called *kyudō*. Kendo is the art of fencing with bamboo staffs.

Gardening is one of the most popular leisure activities in Japan. Many homes have window boxes and a tiny garden, which usually contains sand raked into patterns, a single tree or a rock or two. Bonsai is the traditional art of growing miniature trees. Bonsai trees reach only 30 to 60 centimetres (1 to 2 feet) high. The trees are carefully pruned and wired to make sure the branches grow into a balanced shape. The oldest bonsai trees are more than 200 years old.

In their free time, many Japanese love to shop and go to the cinema and concerts. They also enjoy playing *pachinko*, a pinball game. Karaoke, where people sing along to recorded music, has become popular in many other countries besides Japan. The word 'karaoke' means 'empty orchestra'.

At home, most Japanese people watch television or the latest film on video, practise a musical instrument or listen to music. Reading is another relaxing activity. Besides books, there are about 100 daily newspapers to choose from and thousands of comics and magazines. After the USA, Japan has the second-highest book sales in the world.

Some people visit health clubs throughout the year. For less active people, there are 'mind gyms', where stressed business people go to relax and listen to soothing music while they rest on chairs that sway gently. The Japanese are enthusiastic tourists, although work does not allow much time to take long holidays.

Religion today

The Japanese are a deeply religious people. Ceremonies and rituals lie at the heart of their way of life.

Shinto is the most ancient Japanese religion (see page 49). It has no scriptures like the Christian Bible or the Islamic Koran that give rules about right and wrong. Instead, Shinto teaching emphasizes the importance of believers carrying out simple rituals to cleanse themselves and their things of 'impurities'. Shinto has no concept of sin in the Christian sense; people may become impure when they are ill or are in mourning, for example.

People visiting Shinto shrines purify themselves before entering by rinsing their hands and mouths with water. At the shrine itself, people make an offering of a coin to the *kami* – the spirit of the shrine. On special occasions, gifts of food and drink are offered, or even a sacred dance or a sumo contest are held. Many people visit shrines to pray for good luck.

State Shinto

According to the Shinto religion, ancestors and famous figures from history are gods. In the 1870s, the Japanese emperor established a national religion called State Shinto. It stressed patriotism, or love of country, and revered the Japanese emperor as a god. After World War Two (1939–45), the Allied victors outlawed State Shinto and made the emperor declare that he was not a god.

A Shinto priest adjusts the ceremonial robe of a young man.

The tea ceremony

Chanoyu is the tea ceremony, a ritual that aims to achieve a feeling of peace and harmony and to open the mind for meditation. It began among Buddhist monks in China. The Japanese 'way of tea' was developed by the 16th-century Zen master Sen no Rikyu. In addition to martial arts, samurai warriors studied the tea ceremony.

The ritual draws on both Buddhist and Shinto ideas. It takes place in a beautiful tea garden (see page 99) and can last as long as four hours. At different points in the ceremony, guests admire the garden and the tea house and discuss subjects such as nature, while their host prepares *cha* (green tea; see page 106).

Guests sit Japanese style with their knees bent and their legs tucked under them. The bitter tea is served without sweetener in little cups. After the *cha* has been drunk, the guests admire the beauty of the cups and eat a sweet cake.

Tea masters, like the woman above, train for years to perfect the art of the *chanoyu*. All the objects used – kettle, tea bowls, serving ladle – are chosen especially for their beauty. Even preparing the tea has a set of rules – every move the tea master makes is important and has a meaning. The tea used is powdered green tea, which is made frothy by using a bamboo whisk before serving.

Students pray for good exam results, and business people pray for success at work.

Japan's most important Shinto shrine is at Ise, which lies in a remote area southeast of Nara and Ōsaka. The shrine is sacred to the Shinto sun goddess, Amaterasu (see box). For some 1300 years, the shrine has been demolished and rebuilt every twenty years with fresh timber from the surrounding cypress woods.

Buddhism (see page 52) is as important as Shinto. Most Japanese are both Shintoists and Buddhists and find no contradiction in following both religions. Two particularly popular schools of Buddhism in modern Japan are Zen and True Pure Land.

Zen is a branch of Buddhism that developed in medieval times. It emphasizes the practice of meditation and self-control as the way to inner peace. Zen Buddhism was taken up by samurai warriors (see page 55), who practised meditation to prepare for combat. The martial arts developed by the samurai express Zen ideas. Zen Buddhists also developed the tea ceremony (see box opposite) and the meditation garden.

True Pure Land was an offshoot of an earlier Buddhist sect (group) called Pure Land. True Pure Land teaches that ordinary people can find salvation through simple prayers that are sincerely made. Unlike monks who belong to other, more orthodox (mainstream) Buddhist sects, True Pure Land Monks may eat meat and get married.

Buddhist places of worship are called temples – known as *tera* or *ji* in Japanese (see page 93). The temples are filled with burning incense and the murmur of chants and prayers. Zen monks sit meditating on the ground cross-legged and with their wrists resting on

Amaterasu

The most important god (*kami*) in Shinto is the sun goddess, Amaterasu. According to legend, Amaterasu's brother Susano-ō, who was in charge of the Earth, was jealous of his sister. He made such a noise in the Heavens that Amaterasu fled into a cave, plunging the world into darkness. The other gods coaxed her out of the cave by performing a comical dance with a spear and tempting her with a beautiful jewel and bronze mirror. As soon as the laughing Amaterasu left the cave, sunlight returned.

Amaterasu's grandson Ninigi became the first ruler of Japan. The goddess gave Ninigi three gifts – a sword, mirror and jewel – which became the special treasures of the imperial family.

Zen Buddhists also try to gain enlightenment by meditating on *kōan* (riddles). The most famous *kōan* is 'What is the sound of one hand clapping?'

their knees. To stop them from falling asleep, they are occasionally struck with a bamboo stick.

Many Japanese people also follow the teachings of Confucius, a Chinese philosopher who lived about 500 BC. Few Japanese follow the Christian religion. In cities, however, people sometimes celebrate weddings in a Western-style chapel.

Millions of people follow one of Japan's new religions, of which there are more than 200. Many of these new faiths contain elements of Shinto, Buddhism or Christianity. A Buddhist sect called Sōka Gakkai (Value Creation Society) is a popular new religion, with some 20 million members. Another sect called Aum Shinrikyō (Supreme Truth) believed that the world was going to end in 1997. Aum Shinrikyō became notorious in 1995 when some of its followers released deadly nerve gas on the Tokyo underground. Twelve people died and some 5500 others were injured in Japan's worst terrorist attack.

A calendar of festivals

The Japanese year contains many religious festivals, and there are thirteen national holidays (see box opposite). One of the most important festivals in Japan is held at New Year and is called *Ganjitsu*. On New Year's Eve, the bells ring out to mark the end of the old year. Special decorations made of pine, bamboo and plum-tree branches are placed outside houses. During the New Year celebrations, which continue until 3 January or longer, people visit their families, eat special food and play traditional games. Boys often fly kites, while girls play a game similar to badminton called *hanetsuki*. Many people pay a visit to a Shinto shrine or

Viewing cherry blossoms

During April, parties of office workers and families organize trips to local parks to view the cherry blossoms. Newspapers publish maps to show where the most beautiful blossoms can be found. A particularly popular place in Tokyo to view blossoms is Ueno Park. People picnic under the trees, and there is often music and dancing, too. The custom dates back to the reign of the emperor Saga (809–23).

Buddhist temple, and pray for health and happiness in the coming year.

Girls' Day is on 3 March. Girls visit one another's homes to admire dolls dressed in beautiful kimonos. The festival is also called Peach Day because the graceful flowers of this fruit are associated with girls. May brings Golden Week, when three festivals fall close together, and people have a chance to take a week off. At the end of Golden Week is Children's Day, formerly called Boys' Day, on 5 May. Families with young sons fly paper streamers shaped like carp (see page 99).

Summer festivals include *Tanabata*, the Star Festival, in July. The festival commemorates a princess and a farmhand who were in love but could meet only on one night a year. They are represented by two stars in the sky, the paths of which cross on this night. Children write wishes and tie them to bamboo branches.

At the Buddhist festival of *O Bon*, held in August or July, the spirits of the dead are thought to return to the Earth. People go back to their home towns to visit the graves of their ancestors. They light bonfires and leave food on family graves to greet the spirits. People light lanterns and dance in the streets. August is also a popular month for moon-viewing. At night, small parties of people gather in gardens or on verandas to drink sake and read poetry.

Labour Thanksgiving Day (23 November) originally celebrated the harvest. Today, though, all workers are remembered on this day. The emperor traditionally makes an offering of sake to the gods.

National holidays

1 January	New Year's Day
15 January	Coming of Age Day
11 February	National Foundation Day (see page 47)
20 (or 21) March	Coming of Spring Day
29 April	'Green' Day
3 May	Constitutional Memorial Day (see page 71)
5 May	Children's Day Assumption Day
15 September	Respect-the-Aged Day (see page 117)
23 (or 24) September	Coming of Autumn Day
10 October	Health Sports Day
3 November	Culture Day
23 November	Labour Thanksgiving Day
23 December	Emperor's Birthday (see page 38)

The future

'The Japanese are a great people. They cannot and should not be satisfied with a world role that limits them to making better radios and sewing machines ...'

Singapore prime minister Lee Kwan

Japan has come a long way in the last 50 years. After World War Two (1939–45), Japan's economic recovery was so successful that it was hailed as an 'economic miracle'. In the late 1990s, however, Japan faced new difficulties, including a period of economic slow down. There were other problems, such as overcrowding and an ageing population. In the 21st century, Japan must tackle these problems, especially its financial troubles, if it is to keep its position as a world leader.

ECONOMIC DIFFICULTIES

The 1970s and 1980s were boom years for Japan's economy. Japanese companies grew and prospered and set up factories abroad. Japanese goods were sold worldwide, and the country built up a huge **trade surplus**. Japan's banks and financial institutions became the most powerful in the world.

By the 1990s, Japan's rapid growth was slowing. Japanese factories faced competition from other Asian countries, such as Taiwan and Korea, whose industries had also grown quickly. In about 1992, a period of slow down began to affect countries all over the world. People in many countries had less money to spend on **consumer goods**, so there was less demand for Japanese products. Many Japanese businesses began to struggle. Some downsized part of their workforce; others were forced

Space is a valuable commodity in Japan's cities. The capital, Tokyo, has one of the most densely packed populations in the world.

FACT FILE

● The cities of Tokyo, Yokohama and Kawasaki run almost into each other.

● At the end of the 19th century, Tokyo had a population of about 1 million. Today, with 26 million people, Greater Tokyo is the world's largest city.

● With the success of birth-control methods, Japan has one of the lowest rates of population growth in the world.

● Within ten months during 1990, the Japanese stock market lost 48% of its value.

● Japan has the lowest infant mortality rate in the world.

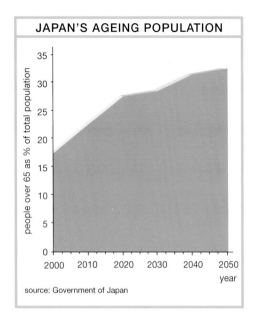

JAPAN'S AGEING POPULATION

people over 65 as % of total population

source: Government of Japan

Experts predict that by 2050, people over 65 will make up almost 35 per cent of the total Japanese population.

to close entirely. The increased use of robots for routine and dangerous jobs in factories put more people out of work. For the first time in many years, unemployment began to rise.

Japan and several of its Asian neighbours entered a time of serious economic difficulty. The value of the Japanese currency fell. Some of Japan's financial institutions collapsed, and others looked less stable than they had for years. The situation also led to political upheaval, and new government leaders came and went.

In 1998, the government announced a series of measures aimed at supporting struggling businesses and boosting the economy. At the same time, European nations, the USA and Japan tried to find ways of stabilizing world markets.

Over the next few years, Japan faces an uncertain economic future. What is certain, however, is that the hard-working Japanese are determined to find solutions to their problems. Because of its lack of **natural resources**, Japan will continue to depend on international trade and pioneer new developments in science and technology. Despite its present troubles, Japan will undoubtedly continue as a dominant force in world trade.

OVERCROWDING

At home, Japan faces the problem of overcrowding. Since the 1950s, cities and factories have grown so rapidly that in many areas, there is now a severe shortage of housing and lack of space.

Some city planners suggest that the answer to this problem is to build higher skyscrapers. This is possibly a dangerous solution in Japan because of the threat of earthquakes. Scientists believe that a major earthquake is now overdue and will strike the east coast of Japan's main island within the next few years. Many experts argue that it would be better to try to solve the problem of overcrowding by reclaiming more land from the sea for factories and new estates.

The government has also encouraged businesses to move away from cities into the countryside. Improvements in technology and communications mean that it is becoming easier for companies to relocate to rural areas and for people to run their businesses from home.

THE 'SILVER GENERATION'

Japan also faces the prospect of an ageing population. As health care improves, people can expect to live longer. At the same time, the birth rate has fallen, with married couples now having only one or two children. Smaller families mean that there will be fewer workers to help support a rising number of old people, known in Japan as the 'silver generation'. Japan is one of the first nations in the world to tackle this problem. With its customary resourcefulness, it is already seeking solutions.

An elderly woman sits reading beneath a cherry tree. Traditionally, the Japanese have valued old age as a time of wisdom and contentment.

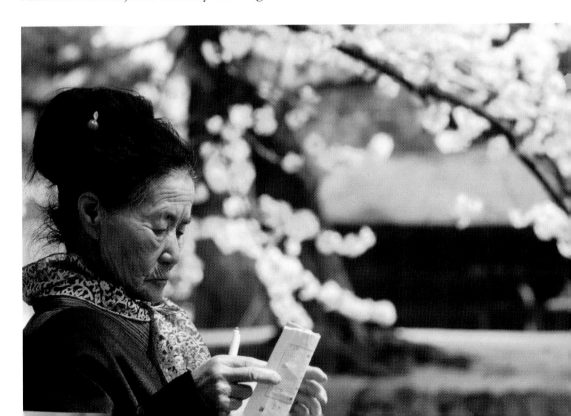

Almanac

POLITICAL

country name:
official form: Japan
local official form: *Nippon/*
Nihon

nationality:
noun: Japanese (singular and plural)
adjective: Japanese

official language: Japanese

capital city: Tokyo

type of government: parliamentary
democracy

suffrage (voting rights): everyone
twenty years and over

independence: 660 BC (traditional)

national anthem: 'Kimigayo' ('Our
Emperor's Reign')

national holiday: 23 December
(Emperor's Birthday)

Flag:

GEOGRAPHICAL

location: eastern Asia; latitudes
30° to 45° north and longitudes
127° to 146° east

climate: ranges from subtropical in
the south to cool temperate
in the north

total area: 377,800 sq km
(145,835 sq miles)
land: 99.2%
water: 0.8%

coastline: 29,800 km (18,500 miles)

terrain: mostly mountainous and
rugged

highest point: Mount Fuji,
3776 m (12,389 ft)
lowest point: Hachiro-gata,
−4 m (−13 ft)

natural resources: fish

land use:
forests and woodland: 67%
arable land: 12%
permanent pastures: 2%
other: 18%

natural hazards: volcanoes and
earthquakes

POPULATION

population (2000): 126.5 million

population growth rate (1995–2000):
0.26%

birth rate (2000): 9.2 births
per 1000 of the population

death rate (2000): 8.3 deaths
per 1000 of the population

sex ratio (2000): 96.1 males per
100 females

total fertility rate (2000): 1.4 children
born per woman in the
population

infant mortality rate (2000):
3.3 deaths per 1000 live births

life expectancy at birth (2000):
total population: 81.5 years
male: 77.8 years
female: 85.0 years

literacy:
total population: 99%
male: 99%
female: 99%

ECONOMY

currency: yen (¥); 1¥ = 100 sen

exchange rate (2003):
£1 = 191¥

gross national product (2000):
£2,717,000 million (second-
largest economy in the world)

gross national product by sectors:
agriculture: 2%
industry: 39%
service: 59%

average annual growth rate
(1990–99): 1.3%

GNP per capita (2000): £21,462

average annual inflation rate
(1990–2000): 0.8%

unemployment rate (1999): 4.7%

exports (2000): £262,000 million
imports (2000): £194,563 million

foreign aid given (2000): £9575 million

Human Development Index
(an index scaled from 0 to 100 combining statistics
indicating adult literacy, years of schooling, life
expectancy and income levels):
92.4 (UK 91.8)

TIMELINE – JAPAN

World history **Japanese history**

c.10,000 BC

c.10,000 Invention of bow and arrow

c.6000 Rice cultivation starts in Asia

c.10,000 Start of the Jōmon culture

c.7000 The world's earliest surviving pottery is made

c.700 BC

551 Birth of the Chinese thinker Confucius

c.563 Birth of the Buddha

221–207 The reign of Qin Shihuangdi, the first emperor of China

c.300 Start of the Yayoi period; rice cultivation, metalworking and the potter's wheel are introduced from China and Korea

c.AD 300

330 Constantinople becomes capital of the Eastern Roman (Byzantine) empire

589–618 The Sui dynasty of emperors reforms China and restores the Great Wall

c.350 Japan is unified under the Yamato clan

c.552 Buddhism is introduced from Korea

592 Prince Shōtoku introduces a legal code and the Chinese calendar

1151 First use of explosives in war by China

1099 The First Crusade captures Jerusalem

1066 Normans conquer England

c.1000

982 Greenland discovered by Erik the Red

800 Charlemagne is crowned emperor of Western (Holy) Roman Empire

639 Muslim armies conquer the southern territories of the Byzantine empire

618–907 China has a 'golden age' of art and literature under the Tang dynasty

c.600

1192 Minamoto Yoritomo becomes the first shogun (military dictator) of Japan. The emperor becomes a figurehead, without real power.

1002 Lady Murasaki completes *The Tales of Genji*

838 Contacts between China and Japan end

794 Heian-kyō (Kyōto) becomes the capital

760 The first great anthology of Japanese poetry – the *Manyoshu* – is collected

710–84 Nara is briefly Japan's imperial capital

681 Date of Japan's oldest historical document, the *Kojiki* ('The Record of Ancient Matters')

c.1200

1215 The Chinese capital, Beijing, falls to the Mongol leader Genghis Khan

1325 Foundation of the Aztec city of Tenochtitlán in Mexico

1368 Foundation of the Ming dynasty in China

1453 Turks capture Constantinople

1492 Columbus lands in America

c.1750 Industrial Revolution begins in England

1274 and 1281 Mongol forces twice invade Japan but are repelled with the help of *kamikaze* ('divine winds')

1467 Long period of civil war begins

1542–43 The Portuguese become the first Europeans to visit Japan

1603 Beginning of the peaceful Edo period

1635 Japan isolates itself from the rest of the world

2000 The West celebrates the Millennium – 2000 years since the birth of Christ

1989 Communism collapses in eastern Europe

1979 Former Soviet Union invades Afghanistan

1969 First man lands on the Moon

1950–53 Korean War

2001 Junichiro Koizumi is elected prime minister of Japan

1995 Kōbe earthquake kills more than 5000

1992 Recession hits economy

1989 Emperor Hirohito dies

c.1960 Japanese economy booms

1947 Japan adopts a new Constitution

c.1945

1945 The USA drops atomic bombs on Hiroshima and Nagasaki; Japan surrenders

1941 Japan bombs Pearl Harbor, bringing the USA into World War Two

1937 Japan launches invasion of China

1905 Japan defeats Russia

c.1800

1804 Napoleon crowns himself emperor of France

1815 French emperor Napoleon is defeated at Waterloo

1839–60 The Opium Wars between China and Britain; China is forced to make huge trading concessions

1853 US Commodore Matthew Perry forces first trading treaty with Japan

1868 The Meiji Restoration – the shogunate is abolished and the emperor is restored to power

1895 Japan defeats China in war over Korea

1949 Communists take power in China

1939–45 World War Two

1933 Adolf Hitler becomes German chancellor

1914–18 World War One

1911 Imperial rule ends in China

c.1900

Glossary

Ainu people thought to be among the earliest inhabitants of Japan

ally country linked to another by a treaty or league

atomic bomb extremely powerful bomb that uses the energy released when the nucleus of an atom is split

Buddhism religion founded by Siddhartha Gautama (the Buddha; about 563–483) that spread throughout central and eastern Asia

bullet trains (Jp. *shinkansen*) high-speed Japanese trains

bunraku (Jp.) traditional Japanese puppet theatre

ceremonial head of state person, such as a king or queen, who represents a nation but holds no real power

chihō (Jp.) name for any one of the nine regions of Japan – for example, Shikoku

coalition alliance between two or more different political groups

conservative political philosophy based on maintaining tradition and stability

constitution fundamental principles that underlie the government of a country

consumer goods manufactured goods ready for sale directly to the public – for example, cars

democracy process that allows the people of a country to govern themselves, usually by voting for a leader or leaders

depression extended slowdown in business activity, during which buying and selling decline and unemployment rises

Edo period peaceful period (1603–1868) in Japanese history when the country was ruled from Edo (later Tokyo) by the Tokugawa family

exports goods sold by one country to another

gross national product (GNP) total value of goods and services produced by the people of a country during a period, usually a year

haiku (Jp.) form of Japanese poetry made up of three lines and seventeen syllables

Heian period period (794–1185) in Japanese history during which the imperial capital was at Heian-kyō (now Kyōto)

imports goods bought by one country from another

industrial(ized) nation country where manufacture is usually carried out with the help of machinery

inflation annual rate at which prices increase

Jōmon (Jp. 'cord marked') name given to the culture of early inhabitants of Japan whose pottery was characterized by cord marks

kabuki (Jp.) colourful and lively form of Japanese drama dating from the late 1600s

kamikaze (Jp. 'divine wind') term first used to refer to the typhoon that hindered a Mongol invasion in 1281. In World War Two, the term referred to Japanese pilots who flew suicide missions.

kanji (Jp.) characters that represent a word or part of a word in written Japanese

ken (Jp. 'prefecture') largest unit of local government in Japan

kimono (Jp.) traditional Japanese garment worn by both men and women, especially during festivals

landscape gardening creation of carefully designed gardens where land is developed for human use and enjoyment

Nara period period (710–84) in Japanese history during which the imperial capital was based at Nara

nationalism people's sense of belonging to a nation; also the belief that a nation should be independent of, and sometimes superior to, other nations

natural resources products and features of the Earth that support life or satisfy people's needs

Noh (Jp.) oldest form of Japanese drama, developed in the 1300s; characterized by formal gestures and tragic subject matter

origami (Jp.) art of folding paper into decorative objects

pagoda tower often found in Buddhist temples

pilgrimage religious journey to a shrine or holy place

Shinto (Jp. 'the way of the gods') oldest surviving religion of Japan, characterized by belief in nature spirits and the importance of ritual purity

shogun (Jp. 'great general') title given to the most powerful of the Japanese warlords

sumo (Jp.) Japanese form of wrestling

sushi (Jp.) popular Japanese dish consisting of elaborately prepared raw fish, rice and vegetables

trade surplus amount of money earned by a country from exports after the cost of imports has been taken away

Zen Buddhism school of Buddhism that teaches that the materials for meditation are found in everyday life

Bibliography

Major sources used for this book
Joseph, J., *The Japanese* (Penguin, 1994)
Kanagawa, D. W. and Erickson, J. Huey, *Japan for Kids* (Kodansha, 1992)
Sanson, G. B., *Japan: A Short Cultural History* (Stanford University Press, 1986)
Seidensticker, E., *Low City, High City* (Harvard University Press, 1991)
Storry, R., *A History of Modern Japan* (Penguin, 1990)
Tasker, P., *Inside Japan* (Penguin, 1990)

General further reading
Clawson, E., *Activities and Investigations in Economics* (Addison-Wesley, 1994)
The DK Geography of the World (Dorling Kindersley, 1996)
The Kingfisher History Encyclopedia (Kingfisher, 1999)
Martell, H. M. *The Kingfisher Book of the Ancient World*. New York: Kingfisher, 1995

Further reading about Japan
Grant, R. G., *Hiroshima and Nagasaki*, 'New Perspectives' (Raintree Steck-Vaughn, 1998)
Hartz, P. *Shinto*, 'World Religions' (Facts on File, 1997)
Herr, M. and Bartok, M., *Ancient Japan*, 'Ancient and Living Cultures' (Goodyear Books, 1992)
Pilbeam, M., *Japan Under the Shoguns*. 'Looking Back' (Raintree Steck-Vaughn, 1999)
Snodgrass, M. E., *Japan and the United States: Economic Competitors*, 'Headliners' (Millbrook Press, 1993)

Some websites about Japan
Japan Information Network
www.jinjapan.org
Japan Search Information
www.japansearch.info/
Japanese Embassy in the UK
www.embjapan.org.uk/
Kids' Japan
www.kids-japan.com
Kids' Web Japan
www.jinjapan.org/kidsweb/index.html

Index

Page numbers in *italics* refer
to pictures or their captions.

A

age, population 10, *118*, 119
agriculture *26*, 27
aikido 55, 110
Ainu 10, 19, 50
air travel 89, *89*
Akihito, Emperor 47, *70*
Amaterasu 51
Andō Hiroshige 95
architecture 37, *37*, 92–3
arts *91*, 92–101
Asakusa 39
Ashikaga Takauji 56
Aum Shinrikyo sect 111

B

baths 104
Beppu 23, 26
birds 31, 32
bombs, atomic 44–5, *45*, 65,
　66–7, *67*
Bonin Islands 13, 27, 69
bonsai 110
books *91*, 110
bowing 103
bridges 25, *25*, 88
Buddhism 11, 25, 39, 52, *52*,
　92, 93, *93*, 99, 111–12

C

car industry 62, *68*, 75, 84
cherry blossom *29*, 30, 112
Chikamatsu Monzaemon 41
Children's Peace Memorial
　44, *45*
Chinese influence 8, 51–2, 91
Christianity 58
chrysanthemums 8, 30
Chugoku 24
cities *15*, 33–45, 51, 72, *83*

Civil Wars, Age of 56, *56*
climate 13, 28–9, *28*, *29*
clothes 104–5, *104*
coastline 13
Confucius 111
Constitution (1947) 71
crafts 100, *100*
cranes, paper 44
crime 7
currency 8, *8*
currents, ocean 28–9

D

daimyō 54, 56, *56*, 57–58
Daisetsuzan National Park
　20, *32*
Dogo Onsen 23
drink 106

E

earthquakes 8, 13, 16, 36, 62,
　62, 70, 93, 118–19
economy 7, 68–70, *68*, 75–89,
　117–18, 121
Edo 33–5, *33*, 57
Edo period 55, 57–8, *57*,
　95
education 107, *107*
emperors 8, 38, 47, 51–3, 65,
　68, 71, 72
energy sources 81, *81*
environmental matters 31–2,
　85
ethnic composition 7, 10, *10*
exports 69, 75, 76, *76*, 77,
　121

F

farming 77–9
ferries 89
festivals 29, 112–13
films 100–1
fishing 31, 79–80, *80*

flag 8
flower-arranging 56, 100
flowers 8, 30
food 8, 80, 105–7, *105*
forests 32, 79
Fuji, Mount 7, 14, 20, *20*,
　21, 22, 94
Fujiwara family 53
Fukuoka 27

G

gardens 56, *91*, 99, *99*, 110
Genghis Khan *54*
government 8, 71–3
Great Kanto Earthquake 36,
　62, *62*
gross national product 7, 75

H

Hachiko 39
haiku poetry 58, 96
health 108, 110
Heian period 53, 91
Hirohito, Emperor 62, 65
Hiroshima 24, 44–5, *44*, *45*,
　65, 66–7, *66*, *67*, 83
history 47–70
Hitachi *83*
Hokkaidō 10, 13, *18*, 19–20,
　19, 28, 30, 78–9
homes *101*, 103–4
Honshū 13, 19, 20–2, 24,
　51, *83*
hotels, 'capsule' 36

I

Ikeda Hayato 69
Imperial Palace *13*, 38
imports 70, 76, *76*, 77, 81,
　121
industry 68, *68*, 69, 75, 82–4,
　85
Inukai Tsuyoshi 63

Isahaya Bay *26*
islands 7, 14, 27, 69, *69*
isolationism 58–9

J

Japanese Alps 20, 22
Japanese Empire 60–5, *61*
Jimmu, Emperor 47
Jōmon 48–9
judo 55, 110

K

kabuki drama 58, 97–8
Kamakura 22, 39, 93
kamikaze pilots 64
Kammu, Emperor 42–3, 53
Kanazawa 24
kanji 8, 11, *19*, *20*, *33*, *40*, *42*, *44*, *49*, *52*, *60*, *62*, *70*, 108
Kanmon Strait 27
karaoke 110
karate 27, 110
Katsushika Hokusai 21, 94, 95
Kawasaki 22, 117
kendo 55, 110
Kitakyushu 27, *83*
Kōbe 16, *18*, *22*, 24, 70, 79, 83, *83*, *88*
Kofun period 51
Korea 60, 61, 68, 86
Kublai Khan 54
Kūkai 25
Kuril Islands 19, 69, *69*
Kyōto 24, 42–3, *42*, *43*, 53, *57*, *83*
kyudō 55, 110
Kyūshū 13, 26–7, *26*, 78

L

lacquer 100, *100*
lakes 17, 24
land use 79
language 11, 50, 102
leisure 109–10
life, everyday 91, 101–13
life expectancy 10, 91, 108
literature 53, 96

M

macaques 31, *31*
Manchuria 61, 62
maps, of Japan *15*, *18*
marriage 91, 101, 103
martial arts 27, *55*, 110
Matsuyama 25
Meiji, Emperor 11, 59, 60, 61
Meiji period 35, 50, 59–61, *60*, 86
Mihara, Mount 17
Minamata Disease 85
Minamoto Yoritomo *53*
mineral resources 81
Mishima Yukio 96
Miya-jima Island 24, *24*
Mongols 54, *54*
monsoons 28
mountains 14, 17, *14*, 20, 21, 26
Murasaki Shikibu 96
music 98, *98*, 110

N

Nagasaki 26–7, 65, *83*
Nagoya 10, 22, 83, *83*
name, of Japan 8, *8*, 52
names 7
Nara 24
Nara period 52–3, 92
Naruto Whirlpools 25
national anthem 11
national holidays 78, 113
national parks 20, 32, *32*
Nikkō 22
novels 96
nuclear power 81

O

Oda Nobunaga 56
oil, crude 81
Okinawa 19, 27, 28, 69
onsen 23
origami 100
Osaka 10, *18*, 24, 40–1, *40*, *41*, 83, *83*, *92*
overcrowding 118–19
overseas visitors 86

PQ

paintings 95, *95*
parties, political 72–3, *73*
Perry, Matthew 59, *59*
place-names 17
poetry 96, 100
pollution 32, 85
Polo, Marco 58
population 7, 9–10, *9*, *10*, 115, 117, 121
ports 89
pottery *49*
prefectures *18*, *19*, 72
puppet theatre 24, 41, 97, 98

R

rail network *60*, 86–7, *87*, 89
regions *18*, 19–27
religion *10*, 11, 49, 52, 58, 111, *111* 113
rice 78, 105
rivers 17
roads *34*, 37, 88, 89
Rykūyū Islands 13, 27, 28, 31, 69

S

Sadako 44
Sakura-jima, Mount 14, *14*, 17
samurai *47*, 54, 55, 58, 100–1, 112
San-yo 24
Sapporo 20, *28*, *83*
sculptures 93
seasons 29
Seikan Tunnel 20
Sendai 21
Shikoku 13, 25, *25*
Shimonoseki 24
Shinto 11, 39, 49, *49*, 52, 91, 92, 111, *111*, 112
shoes 91, 103, 104
shoguns 43, 47, 53, *53*, 56, 57–8
Shōtoku, Prince 52
shrines 24, *24*, 49, 92
Shuto Expressway *34*, 37
silk-farming 79
Sōya Misaki Cape 20

sport 8, 109–10, *109*
springs, hot 22, 23, 26
sumo wrestling 8, 109, *109*

T

Taiwan 60, *86*
Takamatsu 25
tea 22, 106
tea ceremony 56, 112, 113
temples 39, 43, 92, 93, *93*, 99
terrain 7, 14, 17
theatre 41, 97–8, *97*
tidal waves 16
timber 32
Tohoku region 21
Tojo Hideki 65
Tokugawa Ieyasu 35, 43, 57–8
Tokugawa Yoshinobu 59
Tokushima 25
Tokyo 10, 13, *13*, *18*, 22, *28*, 33–9, *33*, 60, 62, 66, 83, *83*,

87, *87*, 89, 114, *114*, 116
torii 24, *24*, 92
towns *15*, 72, *83*
Toyama 24, *83*
Toyota City 22, 75
Toyotomi Hideyoshi 41, 56
trade 69–70, 76, *76*, 77, 81
transportation 25, *25*, 86–9, *87*, 89
trees 30, 32
tsunami 16
tunnels, undersea 20
typhoons 29

U

underground trains *35*, 36, 87
unemployment 86
United Nations 68, 70, *73*

V

volcanoes 13, 14, *14*, 16, 17, *21*, 26

W

whaling 31, 80
wildlife 30–1, *30*, 31, 32
woodblock prints 21, 58, *59*, *60*, 95, *95*
working life 85–6, *86*
World War One 61
World War Two 36, 40, 63–5, 66–7, 68
writing 8, 11, 53, 108

X

Xavier, Francis 58

YZ

yakuza (criminal class) 70
Yamato clan 51
Yayoi 49
Yokohama 10, 22, 33, *62*, *83*, 117

Acknowledgements

Cover photo credit
Corbis: Charles and Josette Lenars

Photo credits
AKG London: 50, 53, 95, 100; **Art Archive:** 33, 46, 67, British Museum 59; National Museum of Tokyo 51; Postal Museum Frankfurt 60; Victoria and Albert Museum 104; **Corbis:** 66; Yann Arthus-Bertrand 37; Bettmann 62; Burstein Collection 21, 94; Lloyd Cluff 16; John Dakers: Eye Ubiquitous 111; Jack Fields 119; John and Dallas Heaton 6; Robert Holmes 23, 90; Hulton-Deutsch Collection 64; Stephanie Maze 101; George McCarthy 30; Charles O'Rear 116; The Purcell Team 25, 71; Roger Ressmeyer 14, 31; David Samuel Robbins 24, 44; Jeffrey L. Rotman 80; Royal

Ontario Museum 49; Michael S. Yamashita 12, 19, 22, 26, 29, 36, 43, 68, 74, 77, 86, 88, 97, 109, 112; **Mary Evans Picture Library:** 98; **Rex Features:** 73; **Tony Stone Images:** 38, 92; Chad Ehlers 84; Charles Gupton 82, 105; Rich Iwasaki 39; Paolo Negri 40; Joel Rogers 99; Pete Seaward 87; **TRH Pictures:** US Army 63; **Werner Forman Archive:** Burke Collection New York 57; L. J. Anderson Collection 55.

Text credit
The publisher would like to thank Alfred A Knopf, a Division of Random House Inc, for permission to reprint the extract on pages 66–7 from John Hersey's *Hiroshima*.